121

TIMED VRITINGS

with *Skillbuilding Drills*

Dean Clayton

Professor Emeritus
University of Arkansas

Sixth Edition

VISIT US ON THE INTERNET
www.swep.com
www.thomsonlearning.com

South-Western
EDUCATIONAL PUBLISHING
Thomson Learning™

Australia • Canada • Denmark • Japan • Mexico • New Zealand • Philippines
Puerto Rico • Singapore • South Africa • Spain • United Kingdom • United States

Business Unit Director: Peter McBride
Executive Editor: Karen Schmohe
Project Manager: Jane Phelan
Editor: Kimberlee Kusnerak
Consulting Editor: Susan Bechtel
Production Manager: Jane Congdon
Manufacturing Coordinator: Carol Chase
Art/Design Coordinator: Michelle Kunkler/Darren Wright
Marketing Manager: Tim Gleim
Marketing Coordinator: Lisa Barto
Cover/Internal Design: Lisa Albonetti Design
Production Services: Cover to Cover Publishing, Inc.

ISBN: 0-538-69240-5

4 5 6 7 WC 03 02

Printed in the United States of America

For permission to use material from this text or product, contact us by
• web: www.thomsonrights.com
• Phone: 1-800-730-2214
• Fax: 1-800-730-2215

Preface

The popular **121 Timed Writings with Skillbuilding Drills** text has been completely revised; it is appropriate for students at any level of keyboarding instruction. The text consists of skillbuilding drills, progressive writings, and timed writings. It can be used (1) as a supplement to any basic keyboarding textbook, (2) as a source of skillbuilding drills and timings, and (3) as an individual skillbuilding program for students with some prior keyboarding instruction but who lack the keystroking power needed for developing strong word processing or production skills. ◄--------------

Organization of the Textbook

The text is organized into two carefully planned and written parts. Part 1 is designed for those with basic keyboarding skills; Part 2 is designed for an intermediate level. Each part consists of three types of drills: technique drills, progressive speed drills, and timed writings.

Skillbuilding Drills:
The technique and fluency drills are designed to refine basic keyboarding techniques in stroking that are essential to developing speed. Strong techniques are the actions that move fingers and hands in the most efficient and effective manner. The more perfect the technique, the faster and more accurately students will key.

To make practice meaningful, students should understand why they are practicing a specific drill. Therefore, each drill is preceded by cues that point out the feature, benefit, and goal for the specific drill and a tip for practicing the drill.

In Part 1, the drills emphasize key locations, specific fingers and rows, the space bar and shift key, weak fingers and adjacent keys that may cause errors, and high-frequency words. The drills in Part 2 emphasize fluency, concentrating on stroking combinations such as balanced-hand and double-letter sequences, common direct and adjacent key reaches, and typical areas of weakness such as opposite-hand errors. Many of the drills correspond to the categories prescribed in the error diagnostic feature of *MicroPace Pro* (see the description that follows).

Progressive Writings:
The popular progressive writings have been given their own section in the sixth edition and more have been added. The progressive writings are an excellent means for motivating students to increase their keyboarding speed and/or accuracy. The timings are designed to be completed in one minute; they range from 20 wam in Part 1 to 96 wam at the end of Part 2. Each paragraph progresses in length by two words. Students should determine their own starting point. When they are able to complete a timing without errors, they are ready to move onto the next speed.

Timed Writings:
The 121 triple-controlled timings progress from easy to average difficulty. All timings are new or have been revised to reflect current content and trends. Timed writing topics address topics of life skills, technology, and workplace readiness. In Part 1, timings are counted as either 2', 3', or 3' and 5'.

All timings are triple-controlled to ensure consistent and reliable results. Extensive research has shown that triple-controlled timed writings help students improve keyboarding skills and provide a consistent measure-

ment of progress. Timings range from easy to average difficulty, with controls for syllabic intensity (SI), average word length (AWL), and high-frequency words (HFW). Easy timings are identified with an *E* for easy or *A* for average.

Word counts and scales throughout the text allow students to check their gross words a minute (gwam) at a glance. See the detailed Timed Writing Instructions that follow on page ix for keying timed writings and computing gwam using the word count columns and scales.

If you are using *MicroPace Pro*, the timings will be checked automatically for speed and accuracy. Each timing may be keyed for a specified number of minutes (1', 2', 3', etc.). Students may also select to practice each paragraph of a timing for 1' and then take a 3' or a 5' writing on the entire paragraph.

Software Support

The 121 timed writings, identified with a clock icon, can be checked by *MicroPace Pro*, a timed writing and skill development software program. The Windows template (ISBN 0-538-69241-3) or the Mac template (ISBN 0-538-69547-1) that accompanies **121 Timed Writings** is required for use with *MicroPace Pro*. The *MicroPace Pro* templates for **121 Timed Writings** each contain

two folders: Writing 1 and Writing 2. The timings in the Writing 1 folder have one space after a period at the end of a sentence. The timings in the Writing 2 folder have two spaces after a period. Copy whichever folder you desire in the *MicroPace Pro* directory/folder. *MicroPace Pro* automatically computes gwam, identifies errors, and provides diagnostic information on each timed writing. Based on the diagnostic report, *MicroPace Pro* then prescribes practice on drills designed to correct the student's most frequent errors.

New to the sixth edition, **121 Timed Writings** is now available with a student version of *MicroPace Pro* (ISBN 0-538-69548-X), which is packaged with the book. The student receives the textbook, the *MicroPace Pro* program disk, and the timings from **121 Timed Writings**.

In Summary

In learning to key, nothing succeeds like success; students must taste of it frequently if they are to continue to grow. Encourage students to maintain a positive and confident attitude in their abilities. Strive to be as relaxed as possible and maintain good techniques.

Dean Clayton

Contents

Part 1
Basic Level Keyboarding

Section A *Skillbuilding Drills*

Section B *One-Minute Progressive Writings* **25**

Section C *Timed Writings*

Two-Minute Timed Writings E

Two-Minute Timed Writings A

Three-Minute and Five-Minute Timed Writings E

Three-Minute and Five-Minute Timed Writings A

Contents

Part 2

Intermediate Level Keyboarding

Section A — Skillbuilding Drills

Section B — One-Minute Progressive Writings   83

Section C — Timed Writings

Three-Minute and Five-Minute Timed Writings Ⓐ

Extended, Five-Minute Timed Writings Ⓐ

Timed Writing Progress Chart

NAME

3' and 5' Timed Writings

Timed Writing Number	Date	Speed	Errors	Length	
				3'	5'
SAMPLE #3	**SEPTEMBER 7**	**28**	**5**	✓	

Progressive One-Minute Writing Chart

Directions: Record the date when you pass a 1' writing without errors.

Gwam	Date	Gwam	Date
20		60	
22		62	
24		64	
26		66	
28		68	
30		70	
32		72	
34		74	
36		76	
38		78	
40		80	
42		82	
44		84	
46		86	
48		88	
50		90	
52		92	
54		94	
56		96	
58		98	

Instructions for Timed Writings

Review the general guidelines for taking timed writings below. Procedures will vary somewhat depending upon the software that is being used. If you are using *MicroPace Pro*, many of the steps are handled automatically. If your software does not keep track of your progress on timed writings, record your results on the chart on pages vii or viii. ◀- -

Preliminary Procedures

1. Use default or 1" side, top, and bottom margins.
2. Use 12-point font.
3. Indent paragraphs 0.5" or to the first default tab.
4. Double-space timings if your software permits.
5. Place the textbook on either side of your computer.
6. Establish proper posture. Keep your elbows close to your body, your fingers curved and hands upright, and your feet on the floor.

If you are using *MicroPace Pro*, steps 1-4 are automatically set electronically.

Guidelines for Timed Writings

1. Key your name, date, and timing number. Double-space to begin the timing. If you are using *MicroPace Pro*, this step is not necessary; this information is printed automatically on each timing.
2. Select a timed writing. Generally, key the easy level, 2' timed writings before progressing to the 3' and 5' writings.
3. If you are using *MicroPace Pro* or a software with a timer, set the timer for the appropriate time and begin when you are ready. If you are using software without a timer, begin keying when the signal is given.
4. Maintain good keying techniques throughout the timed writings.

5. Stop keying when the timer has stopped or when the signal is given.
6. Print the timing.
7. Proofread the timing and circle errors. If your software identifies errors, review them carefully.

> Every word omitted, inserted, misspelled, or in any manner changed from the printed copy is considered an error. Only one error is charged per word. A spacing error following a word is considered to be part of the preceding word.

8. Record your results on the Timed Writing Progress Chart (page vii). Copy the chart as necessary.

Steps in Manually Computing Gross Words a Minute (gwam)

1. Locate the figure in the column at the end of the last complete line keyed. (If two columns of figures are given, be sure to use the appropriate column to compute your gwam.)
2. Locate the figure for the appropriate scale below the paragraph, if a portion of a line has been keyed. Add this figure to the total gwam obtained in step 1.

If you are using *MicroPace Pro*, gwam is computed automatically.

Basic Level Keyboarding

Section A — *Skillbuilding Drills*

General Directions
1. Use default side margins and 12-point font.
2. Single-space drill lines. Double-space between groups of drill lines.
3. Press ENTER after each drill line.
4. Double-space paragraphs; indent each paragraph 0.5".

SKILLBUILDING

Drill 1 •
Alphabetic Sentences

To improve accuracy, key each line once; repeat entire drill. Do not key a number at the beginning of each line.

FEATURE: Each sentence contains every letter of the alphabet.

BENEFIT: Reinforce key locations.

TECHNIQUE TIP: Key steadily. Keep fingers curved and upright, fingertips slightly touching the home keys.

GOAL: One or less errors on each sentence.

1. Janet needs zeal for producing both quality work and excellent volume.
2. Joel Brown quickly organized plans to extend them a formal invitation.
3. Pass by the very unique farm with junk piled next to the grazing cows.
4. You have not acquired zone two except by judgments from marked claims.
5. We just bought the shipment of axes and adzes for a very quick resale.
6. Jim might like to drive this van except for questionable hazy weather.
7. We might quickly develop experience and realize gains from their jobs.
8. The woven fabric in my zippered jacket is gray and exquisitely styled.
9. Students frequently relax for extra vigor and zip to bring on success.
10. Excerpts of videos were recorded by schools in jest for making a quiz.
11. Have workers mark size and quantity on boxed goods for jelly products.
12. We check magazines to best adjust quality of extended policy coverage.
13. Copying examples just before giving a quiz will make students happier.
14. Jack inquired about making the frozen yogurt with extra party flavors.
15. Zak questioned job expenses billed by the newly formed moving company.
16. Boaz is anxious to quickly have justified margins with their computer.
17. Many realize that finding a key job is quite exciting after a preview.
18. Six prize winners are judged as qualified by receiving the most marks.
19. The oranges were squeezed extensively to make pure juice at breakfast.
20. Mickey utilized several required subjects for exploring how to manage.

| | 1 | | 2 | | 3 | | 4 | | 5 | | 6 | | 7 | | 8 | | 9 | | 10 | | 11 | | 12 | | 13 | | 14 | |

TIMED

121. WORD PROCESSING

	gwam 3'	5'

If you are keying this timed writing on a personal computer, `4 | 2 | 88`
you are using some type of word processing software program. `8 | 5 | 90`
These programs generally allow you to format, edit, save, and `12 | 7 | 93`
file documents that you create. As a part of most programs, you `17 | 10 | 95`
are able to work with a table or a graphic. You may use several `21 | 13 | 98`
other tools as you are working with the software program. These `25 | 15 | 100`
programs most likely provide at least these three basic tools-- `30 | 18 | 103`
a spell checker, a thesaurus, and a grammar checker. `33 | 20 | 105`

Based on the kind of word processing software program that `37 | 22 | 107`
is used, a spell checker does not usually have the same name. `41 | 25 | 110`
However, it has the same major purposes--to assist you in locat- `45 | 27 | 112`
ing spelling errors and to assist you in correcting these errors. `50 | 30 | 115`
A spell checker often does more than assist you in working with `54 | 32 | 118`
errors in spelling. It will often point out problems with capi- `58 | 35 | 120`
tal letters, words with numbers, and words that are included more `63 | 38 | 123`
than once. A spell checker often lets you include specific types `67 | 40 | 125`
of dictionaries and to correct spelling errors as you key. `71 | 43 | 128`

The thesaurus is a tool that enables you to search for syno- `75 | 45 | 130`
nyms and antonyms. If you have frequently utilized a thesaurus `79 | 48 | 133`
in book form, you will especially enjoy working with the one pro- `83 | 50 | 135`
vided as a tool in a word processing software program. First, `88 | 53 | 138`
you use the program by choosing a word that you want to replace `92 | 55 | 140`
instead of the word that you keyed. Second, you quickly replace `96 | 58 | 143`
the word from the thesaurus. When not working with a document, `101 | 60 | 145`
you also have an opportunity of only looking up a word. `104 | 63 | 148`

A grammar checker provides an opportunity for proofreading `108 | 65 | 150`
documents for various types of mistakes in the use of grammar. `112 | 67 | 153`
It is often not able to help in finding and in correcting all of `117 | 70 | 155`
the mistakes. However, most of these checkers are fast and thor- `121 | 73 | 158`
ough and worth using. If you wish, you can often select prefer- `125 | 75 | 160`
ences for a checker. For example, a feature may be selected `129 | 78 | 163`
that is closer to your own style of writing. This is often done `134 | 80 | 165`
by selecting one or more styles that are provided on a menu in `138 | 83 | 168`
the checker. You can also develop or add a special dictionary. `142 | 85 | 170`

gwam 3' | 1 | 2 | 3 | 4
5' | 1 | 2 | 3

SKILLBUILDING

Drill 2 •
Alphabetic Paragraphs

To improve accuracy, key a 1' timing on paragraph 1 of each group; determine gwam and mark errors. Repeat using paragraph 2 of each group.

FEATURE: Uses all letters in each paragraph. Paragraphs range from 30-52 words with each paragraph increasing by two words.

BENEFIT: Increase keyboard mastery.

TECHNIQUE TIP: Keep eyes on copy. Concentrate as you key. Keep fingers upright and curved.

GOAL: Two or less errors a minute.

gwam 1'

From the very start good techniques at the keyboard are re-	12
quired. Analyze what you do and adjust at the same quality as	24
for sound physical exercise.	30
Speed is an aspect of keyboarding likely to increase with a	12
very steady rate through practice. Excess stress with control	25
may jeopardize your quantity of work.	32

gwam 1' | 1 | 2 | 3 | 4 | 5 | 6 | 7 | 8 | 9 | 10 | 11 | 12 | 13 |

gwam 1'

Control while keyboarding is not stable. It is usual to	11
have errors when qualified experts are keying. An advent of	24
keying errors is most often recognized as justified.	34
Realize keying numbers is evidently a skill that is justly	12
needed by those using the keyboard. Proper fingers using a quick	25
response are required when keying in the exact numbers.	36

gwam 1' | 1 | 2 | 3 | 4 | 5 | 6 | 7 | 8 | 9 | 10 | 11 | 12 | 13 |

gwam 1'

Some view that the symbol keys need emphasizing just as much	12
as the number keys. Others favor exception to this viewpoint.	25
Specific inquiry appears to stress examples from a computer copy.	38
The quality of good control and increased speed is an index	12
of success. This means you have to work with zeal as you prac-	24
tice. You need joint work on control and on speed, but not at	37
the same time.	40

gwam 1' | 1 | 2 | 3 | 4 | 5 | 6 | 7 | 8 | 9 | 10 | 11 | 12 | 13 |

Drill 2 continued on next page.

Timed Writings
(Extended, 5'-timed writings continued)

120. TYPES OF FIRMS	gwam 3'	5'	

Some major types of firms are those which maintain inventories on the retail level. These types of firms are often referred to as merchandising firms. You most likely purchase goods at several of these firms on a regular basis. Examples of these firms are department stores, food markets, pharmacies, and discount outlets. The size of these firms often ranges from very small to very large. As the cost of inventories is high, it is not easy to begin one of these firms with only limited funds.

A type of firm that also has inventory, but is not like a retail store, is a manufacturer. Finished goods are the inventories sold by this type of firm. The goods of these firms are often sold to wholesalers and large retailers. There is often a difference from one firm to another firm in the type, quantity, and quality of finished goods which are made and sold. Thus, the cost of finished goods on hand at one time will generally vary greatly from firm to firm. In a manufacturing firm, raw materials, labor, and overhead determine the cost of finished goods.

The types of firms that need little, if any, inventory are the service firms. Thus, many service firms are often easier and quicker to start, when compared with most of the other types of firms. You can likely think of differing service firms from whom you have received services. Examples of these firms are cleaning shops, legal offices, clinics, and tax services. In the past few years, the number of service firms has increased at a very rapid rate. The trend is expected to continue in the future.

Firms on the Internet are growing very quickly in our nation today. Only limited funds are needed to build a home page for a web site that sells or promotes products on the Internet. With an increase in use of the Internet, these firms are expected to grow more than other types of firms in the future. Many of these firms are operated from home offices and are very small. However, others are very large. For example, several online firms are listed on the stock exchanges. Older, well-known retail and service firms sell and promote their products on the Internet.

| gwam 3' | 1 | 2 | 3 | 4 |
| 5' | 1 | 2 | 3 |

Timed writings continued on next page.

SKILLBUILDING

Drill 2
(continued)

Proofreading and editing are quite enjoyable when handled   12

properly. Evidence of a skilled person on the keyboard is final   25

copy. Keep analyzing extra means to properly proofread or edit   37

material in final form.   42

Evidence of sizable adjustments in using the keyboard is   11

when you can compose ideas without use of any copy. This is   24

when you can quickly think and key at the same or exact time.   36

Practice using the keyboard to compose.   44

gwam 1' | 1 | 2 | 3 | 4 | 5 | 6 | 7 | 8 | 9 | 10 | 11 | 12 | 13 |

Practice equips you to grow in keyboarding skills. Zoom in   12

on meaningful practice for success in keyboarding. Practice must   25

have an exact purpose before it can produce the correct results.   38

Set major goals and try to reach them.   46

To quickly maximize the best use of your time, do the skill   12

correctly from the beginning. It is much easier to prevent an   25

error than just correct it. Once a pattern is set, it is not   37

easy to change. Know exactly what to do when starting.   48

gwam 1' | 1 | 2 | 3 | 4 | 5 | 6 | 7 | 8 | 9 | 10 | 11 | 12 | 13 |

Because of the widespread use of personal computers, key-   11

boarding is much easier and more exciting. Acquired as widely as   24

pizzas and videos, the personal computer is also a major product   37

that has made keyboarding dominant in the home and the office.   50

Could you pass a quiz about word processing software? Vari-   12

ous types of software are available for use in keyboarding. The   25

most popular word processing software lets you use a personal   37

computer to key in text or printed materials. Know the technical   50

jargon.   52

gwam 1' | 1 | 2 | 3 | 4 | 5 | 6 | 7 | 8 | 9 | 10 | 11 | 12 | 13 |

TIMED

Timed Writings
(Extended, 5'-timed writings continued)

119. WHAT IS ACCOUNTING?	gwam 3'	5'	

Accounting is often referred to as the language of business. | 4 | 3 | 88
For example, assets, liabilities, income, expenses, and other | 8 | 5 | 90
like kinds of terms are recognized by most people who work in the | 13 | 8 | 93
world of business. The accounting process is often fast, easy, | 17 | 10 | 95
and accurate when a computer or a scanning device is used. Some | 21 | 13 | 98
type of computer software is needed for the process to work. Re- | 26 | 15 | 100
gardless of the device that is used for the input, the process | 30 | 18 | 103
has three main steps--to record, to summarize, and to analyze. | 34 | 20 | 105

As the first step in the process of recording is done, a | 38 | 23 | 108
single- or double-entry system of accounting is used. With ei- | 42 | 25 | 110
ther one of these systems, sales, rent, insurance, taxes, and | 46 | 28 | 113
various other items are often recorded. A very small firm is | 50 | 30 | 115
most likely to use the single-entry system. The double-entry | 54 | 33 | 118
system is used in both small and large firms. This system pro- | 58 | 35 | 120
vides for the recording of debits and credits at the same value. | 63 | 38 | 123
Recording is often done in using a computer with accounting soft- | 67 | 40 | 125
ware. Recording provides for the other steps in the process. | 71 | 43 | 128

The second step in the process consists of producing summa- | 75 | 45 | 130
ries of the entries that were recorded during the first step. | 79 | 48 | 133
Although it is helpful to know why and how summaries are pre- | 83 | 50 | 135
pared, a computer quickly and accurately brings together the re- | 87 | 52 | 137
corded items into varied financial summaries. Two of the most | 92 | 55 | 140
commonly used summaries give the condition of a firm at a certain | 96 | 58 | 143
time and the net income of a firm during a period of time. To | 100 | 60 | 145
finish the last step, these and other summaries are needed. | 104 | 62 | 148

Analyzing, the last step in the process, is vital for the | 108 | 65 | 150
well being of a firm. When software with tools for in-depth | 112 | 67 | 152
analysis is used, extensive reports are produced. These reports | 116 | 70 | 155
often include actual versus budgeted items, rate of bad debts on | 121 | 72 | 157
credit sales, net worth changes, and cash flow comparisons. At | 125 | 75 | 160
times, reports are made for two or more years. Another signifi- | 129 | 78 | 163
cant analysis is when the variance in the current assets and the | 134 | 80 | 165
current liabilities of a firm is computed. A report of working | 138 | 83 | 168
capital or current liquid condition of a firm is the result. | 142 | 85 | 170

Timed writings continued on next page.

gwam 3' | 1 | 2 | 3 | 4 |
5' | 1 | 2 | 3 |

SKILLBUILDING

Drill 3 •
Letter-Emphasis
Sentences

Key each sentence once; do not key the letter at the beginning of each line. Repeat drill.

FEATURE: Each sentence contains at least six applications of the letter emphasized.

BENEFIT: Reinforce the location of keys.

TECHNIQUE TIP: Hold hands quiet and reach with fingers. Concentrate on the reaches to letters emphasized in each sentence to improve accuracy.

GOAL: One or less errors on each sentence.

a   An auction at the annual antique sale should attain an ample audience.

b   The baby babbled because a bottle broke on the table before breakfast.

c   The customers created chaos when the car continued to coast and crash.

d   Dates were decided dealing with added funds for decor of the red deck.

e   Employ either one to edit the new eighth edition of the enclosed text.

f   Fine food for the future fair is featured by the factory office staff.

g   Gallon jugs and aged gadgets bring good gains during big garage sales.

h   Humid weather has hindered the hunting and the fishing at the ranches.

i   The items that bring gains in firms may initiate inquiry in investing.

j   Enjoy the jersey jacket or the jeans by just joining our jogging club.

k   Keep kitchen racks stacked with cakes, kale, kumquat, or pumpkin pies.

l   Clubs will label lollipops on the local levels while the public sells.

m   Mistakes are often made if motorists do not remember how to mark maps.

n   We need to notify the news tonight about our next ninth annual picnic.

o   Look your old books over prior to ordering more stock for your stores.

p   Preprint the paper when public opinion polls appear popular to people.

q   The quote on quotas of quality equipment was acquired by your request.

r   Radar revealed that very stormy weather would reach our ranches early.

s   She should submit some arts and crafts from school to several bazaars.

t   The tolls were totaled for the tow trucks at the time of their report.

u   Using our published guides would be quite useful in your four outlets.

v   The visors have several vital ways to improve vision during our visit.

w   Below the wall is their well with pure water drawn near the watershed.

x   A maximum of sixteen extra examples before the next exam is excellent.

y   Always try to quickly study the many ways to go beyond your set goals.

z   Recognize hazy drizzle is a hazard and could jeopardize your own life.

| 1 | 2 | 3 | 4 | 5 | 6 | 7 | 8 | 9 | 10 | 11 | 12 | 13 | 14 |

Timed Writings
(Extended, 5'-timed writings continued)

118. WHAT IS SELF-CONTROL?		*gwam* 3'	5'

	3'	5'
You may consider yourself as a person who appears never to	4	2	88
lose self-control. However, you probably have times when you	8	5	90
lose self-control. You may know others who have very bad tempers	13	8	93
and show them outwardly, while others may control their tempers.	17	10	95
However, it is obvious that lack of self-control is more than	21	13	98
simply having a bad temper. There are various areas of self-	25	15	100
control that you need to consider. For example, do you have	29	18	103
self-control in eating, studying, and watching television?	33	20	105
How does eating identify with self-control? To a great	37	22	107
extent, eating a particular way is usually a habit. Through	41	25	110
self-control, you also know that habits are often changed. How-	45	27	112
ever, they are not easy to change when they develop over a long	49	30	115
period. Eating of junk food, eating at irregular times, and	53	32	117
eating only special types of food are examples of bad eating	57	34	120
habits. Serious health problems may result because of these and	62	37	122
other bad eating habits. A well-balanced diet along with a good	66	40	125
plan of exercise is an example of the use of proper self-control.	70	42	128
Do you apply self-control in your study habits? There are	74	45	130
varied ways to use self-control in performing good study habits.	79	47	133
First, a daily schedule of specific times to study is productive.	83	50	135
Often the schedule is written to serve as a reminder. Second,	87	52	138
all study items should be ready for use at the established time	92	55	140
for study. For example, valuable time is wasted when books,	96	57	143
notes, and related items are not ready for use. Third, designate	100	60	145
a well-lit, quiet location to study so you can concentrate.	104	62	148
Have you wondered if you are watching too much television?	108	65	150
Do you often put off work to watch one or more of your favorite	112	67	153
television programs? If you demonstrate self-control in making	117	70	155
sure that the work is actually completed at a later time, you are	121	73	158
apparently not watching too much television. If you watch pro-	125	75	160
gram after program without any concern for your work, you are	129	78	163
obviously watching too much television. Even if your work is not	134	80	166
involved, you must choose between watching television or doing	138	83	168
some other activity. This is a way of testing your self-control.	142	85	171

Timed writings continued on next page.

SKILLBUILDING

Drill 4 •
Alphabetic Digraphs

To improve speed, key each two-letter combination in color three times before keying the words that follow; then key all sentences one time. Repeat difficult lines.

FEATURE: Two-letter combinations.

BENEFIT: Reinforce key locations.

TECHNIQUE TIP: Concentrate on the letter pairs. Key with quick, snappy strokes.

GOAL: To key two-letter alphabetic combinations with fluency.

a through l

ai air fail hair aim rail said aid/**bi** big bike bit bind bill bite
ca can cake cab scan cat card cap/**de** den aide desk deer dead dent
Can a deer and a cat bite? I can go by air, rail, cab, and bike.

ea eat deal tea ears easy feat earn/**fo** foul foe fort four fox fog
gu gun gulf gust gum gush guy gulp/**ho** hop shop hog show hour hold
Shop for tea and gum. Fog is easy to deal with at the gulf fort.

io ion lion riots action iota junior/**ju** jug junk jury adjust jump
ke key kept lake keg fake kerf keep/**le** led plea leg left let able
Keep a plea before the jury. Key riots led to their able action.

gwam 1' | 1 | 2 | 3 | 4 | 5 | 6 | 7 | 8 | 9 | 10 | 11 | 12 | 13 |

m through z

me met came mean meal come men/**no** nor knot not nod note now known
ou our out pour tout house ouch/**pe** pet pest pen per pent hope pep
Come with me now to our house. You are not pesky or mean per se.

qu quiz quit equip quick quart/**ra** ran rank era rang rash rail rap
se sca scat seal sew case seam/**to** too tour stop told ton toe auto
Stop the quick quiz. Sew the seam in the auto seat and toe seal.

ue due sue blue clue fuel glued/**vi** via view vie movie virus civic
wi wit win wish swim wind wild wig/**xi** exit exist toxic taxi toxin
yo you your yoke rayon yours yon/**ze** zeal zest size zero maze gaze

View the clues in the movie. Do you wish to swim in a wild wind?
The taxi needs fuel. Gaze at the size of the maze. I am amazed.
Rayon is for you. Zest and zeal existed after the toxic viruses.

gwam 1' | 1 | 2 | 3 | 4 | 5 | 6 | 7 | 8 | 9 | 10 | 11 | 12 | 13 |

Timed Writings
(Extended, 5'-timed writings continued)

  A

117. PERSONAL FINANCE SOFTWARE PROGRAMS

	gwam 3'	5'	

In helping to make it easy and fast to deal with personal finances, there are various software programs on the market for use with the personal computer. The programs help a person keep up with investments, plan for retirement, prepare for filing tax forms, and work with other kinds of tasks that relate to money. A person often uses these programs to invest and bank online. However, three basic uses of these programs are to make budgets, keep records of income and expenses, and prepare reports.

Budgets are most often made on a monthly basis for a period of one year. Income and expense items are estimated in a budget. Examples of personal income items are salary, tips, interest, and dividends. Examples of personal expense items are rent, clothes, auto, and income taxes. As income and expense items are often not the same from person to person, budget items will vary. When a current budget is made, budgets from one or more prior years are often helpful. Software programs for personal finance provide a quick way to move and change varied items in a budget.

To keep a record of income and expense items that occur, a software program for personal finance is useful. A record of each income and expense item is keyed in a register with the personal computer. Checks, deposits, and electronic bank transfers are the most common items entered in a register. Most programs allow a person to key an actual check or deposit slip with the use of a personal computer. The content of the check or deposit slip is then in the register without any more keying.

Once a budget is made and all items are in the register, reports of varied kinds are quickly and easily created with the software program. For instance, a bank statement is very quick and easy to reconcile if all checks, deposits, and electronic transfers are entered accurately. Reports by the month, by the year, or for any other period of time are also quick and easy to prepare with use of the program. Some of the kinds of reports, either in figures or graphs, are cash flow, comparison of actual and budgeted items, and separate income and expense items.

gwam 3' 5' gwam values per line (3' | 5' | cumulative):
4 | 2 | 88
8 | 5 | 90
13 | 8 | 93
17 | 10 | 96
21 | 13 | 98
25 | 15 | 101
30 | 18 | 103
34 | 20 | 106
38 | 23 | 108
42 | 25 | 111
46 | 28 | 113
51 | 30 | 116
55 | 33 | 118
59 | 36 | 121
64 | 38 | 124
68 | 41 | 126
72 | 43 | 129
76 | 46 | 131
80 | 48 | 133
84 | 50 | 136
88 | 53 | 138
92 | 55 | 141
97 | 58 | 144
101 | 61 | 146
105 | 63 | 148
109 | 65 | 151
113 | 68 | 153
117 | 70 | 156
121 | 73 | 158
126 | 75 | 161
130 | 78 | 163
134 | 81 | 166
139 | 83 | 169
142 | 85 | 171

Timed writings continued on next page.

gwam 3' 5' | 1 | 2 | 3 | 4 |
| 1 | 2 | 3 |

SKILLBUILDING

Drill 5 •
Alphabetic Trigraphs

To improve speed, key each three-letter combination in color three times before keying the words that follow; then key all sentences one time. Repeat difficult lines.

FEATURE: Common three-letter combinations.

BENEFIT: Reinforce the location of keys.

TECHNIQUE TIP: Concentrate on the letter combinations. Keep fingers curved and wrists low.

GOAL: To key three-letter combinations with fluency.

a through l

ate rated late stated fate dated/**bea** beat bears beads beach beans
cir circles circus circuit cirrus/**der** derby deride dermis derives
The bears are late to the circus.   I beat him in the beach derby.

eat eatery beat neatly feat heat/**fir** fire firm firing firth first
gas gasp gash gasket gassy gasps/**has** haste hash hasty hasp hasten
He is first to eat at the eatery.   Neatly heat a gasket in haste.

ide ides hide abide idea aide bide/**joi** join joints jointed joiner
kin kind kindle king kindly kink/**lon** lone long clone alone lonely
The idea is to hide the king.   We are alone in that lonely joint.

gwam 1' | 1 | 2 | 3 | 4 | 5 | 6 | 7 | 8 | 9 | 10 | 11 | 12 | 13 |

m through z

men mends mental menus mentors/**nor** norms abnormal snores northern
ord order ordeal records cord/**ple** pled ample plenty simple please
Mentors had plenty of records for norms.   Order two simple menus.

qua quay quail quaint quark quarts/**rea** real ream ready rear realm
sin sine since sing single sink/**ton** tons tonight tone baton toner
Are you ready to sing with a baton tonight?   Buy quarts of toner.

und undo under fund undue sundry/**ven** vend vendors vena venom vent
whi whiz while white whirs which whirl/**xyl** xylene xylems xylidine
yea yeah yeast years yearns yearly/**zip** zips zippers zipping zippy

Do you yearn to understand the words xylene, xylem, and xylidine?
While vendors have sundry yearly income, they are in a big whirl.
The vendor may be so underfunded, but is zippy from year to year.

gwam 1' | 1 | 2 | 3 | 4 | 5 | 6 | 7 | 8 | 9 | 10 | 11 | 12 | 13 |

Extended, Five-Minute Timed Writings

116. BUYING A HOUSE

gwam 3' | 5'

Although some people may prefer to rent a house, others may | 4 | 2 | 88
prefer to buy one. For instance, people who intend to remain in | 8 | 5 | 90
one geographic area for a short time often prefer to rent. How- | 13 | 8 | 93
ever, others who plan to remain in one geographic area for a long | 17 | 10 | 96
time often prefer to buy. In some cases, renting or buying is a | 21 | 13 | 98
matter of personal preference. Before buying a house, a person | 26 | 15 | 101
should make some important decisions. Three of these decisions | 30 | 18 | 103
often include location, features, and financing of a house. | 34 | 20 | 106

The location of a house is probably the most important con- | 38 | 23 | 108
sideration when buying. To have the most desirable location, | 42 | 25 | 110
some persons choose to take a longer time to commute or drive to | 46 | 28 | 113
their jobs. The neighborhood, including zoning regulations, is | 50 | 30 | 116
also important in locating a house. The size of the house and | 55 | 33 | 118
the lot on which it is located should also meet the special needs | 59 | 35 | 121
of the buyer. When available, a small acreage is often a good | 63 | 38 | 123
location for a house. Regardless, a thorough study of the area | 67 | 40 | 126
for locating is often needed to predict potential gain in value. | 72 | 43 | 128

Although the square footage of a house is an important fea- | 76 | 45 | 131
ture, the quality of a structure is also very important. For | 80 | 48 | 133
example, a buyer often notes outside framing, insulation, plumb- | 84 | 50 | 136
ing, and electrical wiring. A new house often has a warranty, | 88 | 53 | 138
while one that is not new most likely does not. Thus, the cost | 92 | 55 | 141
of hiring a professional to inspect a house that is not new is | 97 | 58 | 143
most often money well spent. When buying a house, good land- | 101 | 60 | 146
scaping and up-to-date improvements are important features. | 105 | 63 | 148

Most houses are financed through some kind of agency that | 108 | 65 | 150
specializes in providing home loans. Like shopping for a house, | 113 | 68 | 153
it is vital to shop for the best home loan on the market. Inter- | 117 | 70 | 156
est rates may vary from one agency to another. At first glance, | 121 | 73 | 158
a small difference in interest rates may seem unimportant. After | 126 | 75 | 161
computing the interest over the life of a long-term loan, there | 130 | 78 | 163
is often a significant variation. A down payment, along with a | 134 | 81 | 165
good credit rating, is frequently essential before a long-term | 138 | 83 | 168
loan is consummated with an agency that makes home loans. | 142 | 85 | 171

Timed writings continued on next page.

gwam 3' | 5' | 1 | 1 | 2 | 2 | 3 | 3 | 4

SKILLBUILDING

Drill 6 •
Specific Fingers/Rows

Single-space each group of drills; double-space between groups. Repeat the drill.

FEATURE: Emphasizes a specific finger or a specific row.

BENEFIT: Reinforce key locations and stroking techniques.

TECHNIQUE TIP: Reach to the first and third rows with minimum hand movement.

GOAL: To improve stroking techniques.

First Finger

notify forth mover hymn tying right buyer month height gym bright
but my/night job/have fun/hurry home/much more/from the/very true
Your future venture might not be hard to judge when you buy them.

Second Finger

cider edit deck deed dock did die keep check kid kick dicker idea
kind deed/check it/keen idea/code red/dig deep/deck key/we agreed
Did he decide to check and see if his key is behind the red deck?

Third and Fourth Fingers

solo loss slow low six was wall looks poll pool local pizza spool
so soon/was slow/low solo/looks will/was lost/six pales/pool wall
Quietly wait for local pool spots to sell pizza at six locations.

Bottom Row

ax cab name banana cave zone mine back voice number man maze exam
many can/move back/voice box/main exam/exact number/vacant cabins
Maxi can excel by coming back to examine the mice move in a maze.

Second Row

hall gas dad has staff half fad glad shall flag glass flash false
all day/dad ask/glass jar/had half/shall fade/safe as/add alfalfa
Karl shall add a dash of sage and a dash of salt to half a salad.

Third Row

quote report were port riot error trip tree quit wire worry write
were we/put up/wire it/report error/our pie/you worry/wrote witty
We quit to write our tour trip report while you were at the port.

Fourth Row

Code 18759/Model 24638/Building 09762/Lot 34851/Project 467912853
Obtain Order 465230 at bin 8719 with the Catalog No. 01923874651.
The phone card No. 8426730519 and phone No. 555-570-1324 are new.

gwam 1' | 1 | 2 | 3 | 4 | 5 | 6 | 7 | 8 | 9 | 10 | 11 | 12 | 13 |

TIMED

Timed Writings
*(3'- and 5'-timed
writings continued)*

A

114. CORPORATE BONDS
gwam 3'

Bonds of a company may carry a mortgage or a lien to further	4 / 51
protect a purchaser of the bonds. The interest rate is routinely	9 / 55
printed on the face of the bonds. Bonds, unlike stocks, carry an	13 / 59
interest rate regularly payable on a periodic basis to the bond-	17 / 64
holders. When sold, bonds may be discounted or purchased at a	21 / 68
premium ascertained by the credit rating of the company or the	26 / 72
market value of the current interest rates. Bonds are often a	30 / 76
useful way for a corporation to raise funds. Bonds are often	34 / 80
less risky than stocks. Thus, the income from bonds is not usu-	38 / 85
ally as great as the dividends and growth of stock. However,	42 / 89
most experts advise holding both stocks and bonds for investment.	47 / 93

gwam 3' | 1 | 2 | 3 | 4 |

115. JOB ANNOUNCEMENTS
gwam 3' | 5'

Do you know how vital it is for a firm to announce and fill	4 / 2 / 47
a position? To secure the best person, a firm should plan to	8 / 5 / 50
advertise the position where the applicants are most likely	12 / 7 / 52
located. Varied means are used for advertising a position. Ex-	16 / 10 / 55
amples are newspapers, periodicals, direct mail, and the Inter-	21 / 12 / 57
net. In the notice of a vacancy, some of the parts are the job	25 / 15 / 60
title, the job description, the salary, the education and work	29 / 17 / 62
experience, the references, and the closing date to apply. The	33 / 20 / 65
announcement should be in a neat, well-arranged format.	37 / 22 / 67
Most firms interview candidates prior to hiring them. The	41 / 25 / 69
interview is often conducted by a committee. Whether one person	45 / 27 / 72
or a committee interviews, initial work must be done by a firm to	50 / 30 / 75
ensure the right questions are asked in an interview. If any	54 / 32 / 77
data about the education and work experience of the person are	58 / 35 / 80
needed, references and others who know the candidate are often	62 / 37 / 82
contacted. To have success in hiring the right person, both the	66 / 40 / 85
firm doing the hiring and the person hired should feel excited	71 / 42 / 87
about the decision. If this is not true, both parties may lose.	75 / 45 / 90

*Timed writings contin-
ued on next page.*

gwam 3' | 1 | 2 | 3 | 4 |
5' | 1 | 2 | 3 |

SKILLBUILDING

Drill 7 •
Weak Fingers/
Opposite Hand

To improve reaches with weak fingers and opposite hands, key each line once. Repeat difficult lines.

FEATURE: Emphasizes keying with weak fingers or combinations keyed with opposite hands.

BENEFIT: Strengthen weak fingers. Reduce errors on opposite-hand reaches.

TECHNIQUE TIP: Hold hands, wrists, and elbows quiet when reaching with the outside fingers.

GOAL: To maintain fluency with minimal hand and arm motion.

Weak Fingers

sample equip quiz pale zip acquire ax panel power amaze has awake
experts walk soap pass aqua wasp apply zebra load lazy quail also
quote ask wall plow maximize equation dozen examples pay as paper

was amazed/secure pay/pass quiz/seize power/wax cars/place quotes
lazy zebras/appear happy/also explain/aqua wall/has paper/we will
maximize load/dozen examples/quickly aware/apple prices/tall size

Will plaster exhibits at extra bazaars quickly draw local crowds?
Now we expect to park police squad autos in bronze or aqua zones.
How do we explain these qualities of zeal, will, poise, and zest?

gwam 1' | 1 | 2 | 3 | 4 | 5 | 6 | 7 | 8 | 9 | 10 | 11 | 12 | 13 |

Opposite Hand

word believe rush city night known either rust type sleeve height
run witty slide society right tow achieve rubber quality bow slip
now urgent duty slope light mower receive rule sixty sight growth

believe their/known either/usual height/now achieve/receive mower
urgent duty/right quality/run forward/snowy city/bow tie/slide to
slight growth/witty words/busier society/slight rust/higher goals

You might receive urgent word tonight from the busy city council.
A friend knows future towns are sixty to seventy miles up slopes.
I view slight growth as worthy and of high quality and structure.

Should you explain the right rules at their sleigh party tonight?
Al decided to check with them for the codes to the main entrance.
If the audits show problems, the profits at this time are dismal.

gwam 1' | 1 | 2 | 3 | 4 | 5 | 6 | 7 | 8 | 9 | 10 | 11 | 12 | 13 |

Timed Writings
*(3'- and 5'-timed
writings continued)*

112. CORPORATE STOCKS

gwam 3'

A corporation very often has two major stocks, common stock	4	50
and preferred stock. Transfer of these stocks may take place	8	54
through major stock exchanges, over the counter, or through a	12	58
corporation. Stocks often differ in rights assigned to them.	17	63
For example, common stock provides the buyer with an opportunity	21	67
to vote, but it does not return a set rate for the dividends.	25	71
Preferred stock does not provide for voting, but it does return a	29	75
set rate for its dividends. A dividend must be declared before	34	80
it is paid to those who are the holders of the stock. In addi-	38	84
tion to earnings from dividends, two other major purposes of hold-	42	88
ing stock are for growth and as a hedge against inflation.	46	92

gwam 3' | 1 | 2 | 3 | 4 |

113. TELECOMMUNICATIONS

gwam 3' | 5'

How we communicate has come a long way since the first tele-	4	2	48
graph. The word "telecommunications" describes how we send mes-	8	5	50
sages over a long distance. You can communicate from one place	12	7	53
to another by the electronic transmission of signals. Devices	17	10	56
that can send such signals include the cable, the telephone, the	21	13	58
radio, and the television. A very quick and effective way to	25	15	61
communicate is by the use of audio and video. A video conference	30	18	63
call instead of a meeting is easy to plan and can save money, as	34	20	66
it reduces travel costs. Persons can see and hear each other.	38	23	68
The computer and the satellite have made great changes in	42	25	71
how we communicate. E-mail messages sent by use of a computer	46	28	73
modem are very common in many firms. Computers may be used for a	50	30	76
meeting that may take place in various locations outside a firm	55	33	78
or only within a firm. A computer terminal is needed at each	59	35	81
location. The same type of meeting with video is also possible	63	38	83
by using a satellite to send messages from one place on earth to	67	40	86
another place on earth. You will be sure to see more changes as	72	43	89
old communication systems are updated with digital technology.	76	46	91

*Timed writings contin-
ued on next page.*

gwam 3' | 1 | 2 | 3 | 4 |
5' | 1 | 2 | 3 |

SKILLBUILDING

Drill 8 •
Shift Key and
Caps Lock

To improve accuracy, key each line once; rekey any lines in which you had one or more errors.

FEATURE: Emphasizes the shift key and/or caps lock.

BENEFIT: Improve control of shift key and caps lock.

TECHNIQUE TIP: Use a quick "one-two" stroking rhythm.

GOAL: One or less errors on each line.

Right Shift Key

The West-Star Rodeo is held yearly in Tulsa at the end of August. Wes and Dave plan to travel to Rain Springs, Tennessee, in April. The Redbud Choir will sing at the South Shopping Center tomorrow.

Left Shift Key

Jo Lock is scheduled to work at Northern Union Lodge each Monday. Nate plans to walk in the Hally Halloween Parade at Jackson Mall. Please attend the opening of the Ole-Kings Lobster House in June.

Both Shifts

Alan Beth Clay Doris Than Fran George Helena Incan Julie Ken Lane Marion Nan Oscar Peggy Quint Ruth Steven Ulene Victor Wanda Xamie Yelson Zena Thai Opal Sam Paula Sherman Katy Earl Jane Frank Jill

Al can go to the Pike County Court House before the court in May. Coach Nix from Web High School was interviewed on Monday at noon. North Gulf Bay is the site for the new Kyle School of Journalism.

gwam 1' | 1 | 2 | 3 | 4 | 5 | 6 | 7 | 8 | 9 | 10 | 11 | 12 | 13 |

Caps Lock

KWXY, WOPR, and WHYE want longer hours than WILO, KIMQ, and KIOP. These relate to a computer: RAM, CD-ROM, WAV, LAN, DVD, and MCI. MD, RN, and LN are medical terms; CPA and MBA are business terms.

MR. JOSEPH HUNTLEY is located on SUNSET DRIVE in JAMIS, MICHIGAN. MS. MARY SCOT works at BAKER MEDICAL SUPPLIES in CLARK, ARKANSAS. MRS. GERALD MARSHALL lives on SOUTH NORGE STREET in RIPLEY, IOWA.

gwam 1' | 1 | 2 | 3 | 4 | 5 | 6 | 7 | 8 | 9 | 10 | 11 | 12 | 13 |

TIMED

Timed Writings
(3'- and 5'-timed writings continued)

110. RETAINING EMPLOYEES

gwam 3'

One of the most important ways to retain employees is by 4 | 50
fair treatment. If a worker does not perform well because of a 8 | 55
problem on the job, the employer needs to treat the employee 12 | 59
fairly in trying to solve the problem. It is likely that during 17 | 63
the tenure of an employee some kind of problem may occur. If a 21 | 67
problem does occur, the employee needs to know what the problem 25 | 71
is and how it may be solved. A meeting between the employer and 29 | 76
the employee about the problem should be held. After a meeting, 34 | 80
it is often best for the employer to describe the problem in 38 | 84
writing. When applicable, a list of suggestions for improvement 42 | 89
is helpful. The employee should have access to this information. 46 | 93

gwam 3' | 1 | 2 | 3 | 4 |

111. BUSINESS LOANS

gwam 3' | 5'

A business often needs loans for short periods of time. In 4 | 2 | 47
this case, a bank is probably the best source. Interest is fre- 8 | 5 | 50
quently higher for short-term loans than for long-term loans, but 13 | 8 | 52
the mode of obtaining the funds is normally quicker. Firms often 17 | 10 | 55
have a line of credit that will not impose any mortgage on prop- 21 | 13 | 58
erty for short-term loans. This is especially the situation when 26 | 15 | 60
a business has acquired an excellent credit rating, which is 30 | 18 | 63
essential for a firm requiring short-term loans. However, a 34 | 20 | 65
mortgage is usually required if there is not a line of credit. 38 | 23 | 68

Long-term loans for a firm extend over a long period of 42 | 25 | 70
time. For example, ten to twenty years is very common. Firms 46 | 28 | 72
very often make long-term loans to acquire land, buildings, ma- 50 | 30 | 75
chinery and equipment, and related items with extended life. It 54 | 33 | 77
may be necessary to obtain a mortgage on the items purchased plus 59 | 35 | 80
other items owned by a firm. Corporations might wish to issue 63 | 38 | 83
more stocks to obtain funds for long-term purchases. However, 67 | 40 | 85
the sale of bonds by a corporation is another popular means of 71 | 43 | 88
raising long-term funds with loans from bondholders. 75 | 45 | 90

Timed writings continued on next page.

gwam 3' 5'

Drill 9 •
Adjacent Keys

Key each set once; repeat the set; work for accuracy.

FEATURE: Side-by-side keys that often cause errors.

BENEFIT: Decrease common keystroke errors.

TECHNIQUE TIP: Think as you key. Keep fingers upright, not slanting over the keyboard.

GOAL: To key letters adjacent to each other with proper fingers.

we/ew

weed drew web sew weave ewe wed pew well dew wedge rewards wealth
we knew/news weekly/twenty crews/weather grew/were viewed/wet ewe
Few welcomed news that we went to work on the new crew last week.

er/re

other reach where recent nerve before together sure every review
remain there/are here/were over/per reply/her stores/offers more
Orders of computer credit reports are reviewed by buyers for her.

ds/ui

trends built stands quick fields equips goods quiet sounds liquid
ads require/methods quiz/friends acquire/liquid loads/built roads
Funds quite often require records to build ads in acquiring bids.

gwam 1' | 1 | 2 | 3 | 4 | 5 | 6 | 7 | 8 | 9 | 10 | 11 | 12 | 13 |

gwam 1'

Numerous adjacent keys occur in these paragraphs. Strive for continuity and control. Key a 1' timing on each paragraph and mark errors.

As people join different career fields, important opportuni- 12
ties and new situations are encountered. Inquiry into open posi- 25
tions represents an important ingredient. Once an open position 38
is discovered, an application form is frequently requested. A 50
recent resume and a list of previous experience are very often 63
required with an application letter. 70

When you are considered for a position, an interview may 11
emerge. Two personal prerequisites before an interview are often 25
salary and other contract policies. Discovering the prerequi- 37
sites prior to the interview is not always possible. Therefore, 50
asking about such prerequisites may be required. However, in- 62
quire quietly about salary and rewards. 70

Drill 9 continued on next page.

gwam 1' | 1 | 2 | 3 | 4 | 5 | 6 | 7 | 8 | 9 | 10 | 11 | 12 | 13 |

Timed Writings
(3'- and 5'-timed writings continued)

108. EMPLOYEE BENEFITS

gwam 3'

An employee of a firm is one of its greatest resources.	4 50
Formal ways to protect each employee are planned by a firm. Good	8 55
working conditions as well as employee benefits are needed. Some	13 59
of the common employee benefits are varied kinds of insurance	17 63
programs including health, life, disability, and unemployment.	21 67
Some of the costs for these programs are shared by both the em-	25 71
ployer and employee. Also, a firm often helps with a sound re-	29 76
tirement program. In this program, income of the employee is	33 80
often not taxed until the proceeds start. This kind of program	38 84
helps an employee plan for the future. It also gives an employee	42 88
a good reason to remain with a firm over a long period of time.	46 93

gwam 3' | 1 | 2 | 3 | 4 |

109. KINDS OF ADVERTISING

gwam 3' | 5'

There are several approaches firms and other groups take	4	2 48
when advertising their goods and services, as well as different	8	5 50
ways to deliver their advertising. One of the most popular is an	13	8 53
ad that aims at the direct selling of certain goods or services	17	10 56
to a customer. This kind of advertising is an attempt to per-	21	13 58
suade persons to quit using or to keep using certain goods or	25	15 60
services. This kind of advertising is often used to sell or to	29	18 63
promote new or unknown goods or services to the public. For the	34	20 66
most benefit, this kind of advertising must use the right media.	38	23 68
Institutional advertising is also a well-known kind of ad-	42	25 70
vertisement. Rather than trying to sell the concept of buying a	46	28 73
specific good or service, this kind of advertising promotes a	50	30 76
good or a service in general. The florist, book, dairy, and beef	55	33 78
associations are examples of advertisers of this nature. This	59	35 81
kind of advertising is not limited to an association; some firms	63	38 83
may prefer to stress the general services and concepts that they	67	40 86
have. Note that this type of advertisement does not try to sell	72	43 89
a single brand, but persuades people to buy a type of product.	76	46 91

Timed writings continued on next page.

gwam 3' 5' | 1 | 2 | 3 | 4 |

Drill 9
(continued)

To improve accuracy, key the drill lines; key a 1' timing on each paragraph and mark errors. Strive for control.

rt/tr

art extra effort trust fourth try heart street start trade depart
district court/start trip/party tray/extra portions/fourth street
Extra articles advertise further control of north trade industry.

io/oi

choice lotion invoice nation foil various noise prior voice radio
prior point/doing various/joint election/motions void/joins riots
Prior joint union actions to choice oil stations voice divisions.

op/po

post proper power copy purpose hope report stop pond opinion port
post option/report topic/open deposit/operates power/proper point
The report copy opts to oppose the positive options for a choice.

as/sa

ask sand ideas sauce fast said assure saves cash message was sale
saves assets/safety assists/sample ideas/cash sales/last messages
The basic sample has satisfied a basis for the class essay ideas.

gwam 1' | 1 | 2 | 3 | 4 | 5 | 6 | 7 | 8 | 9 | 10 | 11 | 12 | 13 |

gwam 1'

Two considerations frequently guide people to purchase a 11
new computer. One consideration frequently required is to deter- 24
mine your needs. You may opt to request opinions about computer 37
purchases made by friends. Users with related needs are the peo- 50
ple to ask. If you have rare requirements, an expert may impart 63
advice to serve these needs. 69

Another frequent consideration results from inquiries con- 11
cerning the kinds of options open to you. These options are dem- 24
onstrated by previous owners, sales representatives, and other 37
experts in the area. Recent articles, sales reports, and various 50
advertisements serve as important guides. Requesting information 63
from manufacturers may help. 69

gwam 1' | 1 | 2 | 3 | 4 | 5 | 6 | 7 | 8 | 9 | 10 | 11 | 12 | 13 |

Timed Writings
(3'- and 5'-timed writings continued)

  A

106. BANKING SERVICES

gwam 3'

A bank is probably the most common financial institution | 4 | 49
that a firm will use. You should recognize that a bank is a | 8 | 53
business that is formed to earn profits. Banks serve small to | 12 | 58
large firms. A checking account and a line of credit for short- | 16 | 62
term loans are two of the primary services a bank provides a | 20 | 66
firm. Also, a bank provides real estate loans and other loans on | 25 | 70
equipment and machinery that are frequently long term. Other | 29 | 75
services that banks frequently provide to a firm are depositing | 33 | 79
of checks and renting of safety deposit boxes. Banks also pay | 37 | 83
interest on certain types of accounts and certificates of de- | 41 | 87
posit. You need to shop around for the best banking services. | 46 | 91

gwam 3' | 1 | 2 | 3 | 4 |

107. WAYS TO FORM A FIRM

gwam 3' | 5'

A partnership is a common way of forming a firm. At times | 4 | 2 | 48
there is a tax saving when one is a partner instead of a sole | 8 | 5 | 50
proprietor. By filing the right papers, a small partnership may | 12 | 7 | 53
elect to be taxed as a corporation and pay income tax in this | 17 | 10 | 55
manner. Partners may also wish to incorporate because of the | 21 | 12 | 58
limited personal liability that each one will experience if legal | 25 | 15 | 61
claims are made by others. Also, it is often the case that fami- | 29 | 18 | 63
lies will form partnerships when their goals are compatible. | 33 | 20 | 66
Forming a partnership is often easier than forming a corporation. | 38 | 22 | 68

Corporations are very popular types of business firms. | 41 | 25 | 70
Small corporations can pay income tax as partnerships, if they | 46 | 27 | 73
prefer to do so. As one might guess, larger firms are often | 50 | 30 | 75
formed as corporations rather than partnerships. As a firm gets | 54 | 32 | 78
larger or a parent company forms, it is often important to incor- | 58 | 35 | 80
porate to maintain the proper levels of control. One of the most | 63 | 38 | 83
common reasons for forming a corporation is its limited liability. | 67 | 40 | 86
If a case is lost that includes money, the assets of the corpora- | 72 | 43 | 88
tion are subject to claims. A holder of the stock is not liable. | 76 | 46 | 91

Timed writings continued on next page.

gwam 3' 5'

SKILLBUILDING

Drill 10 •
High-Frequency Words

Part A
To increase your speed, key each of the four groups of drills. Repeat as time permits.

FEATURE: Commonly used words.

BENEFIT: Build fluency on commonly used words.

TECHNIQUE TIP: Keep fingers curved and upright over the keys; wrists low.

GOAL: To key the words with fluency.

First 100 Words

thank copy about now please work also been if use most and letter service for these from when company all order very years time our each have office but two many who had any that only department so

some know he I not in by at his them year would we no an on which they one program you more are of be such information were us like am make your this should out than up will new is enclosed was may

with can has there the as two their other do or made to my it may business me appreciate been years in only program like please the each a this most company our be from an most all many them of new

gwam 1' | 1 | 2 | 3 | 4 | 5 | 6 | 7 | 8 | 9 | 10 | 11 | 12 | 13 |

Second 100 Words

through since how part again meeting days help number price above into area used school every during call next let three being line before present its take wish opportunity after much city same see

policy need matter amount percent state just under received could material over shall cost form however get mail special way people send date first well due month plan necessary those hope day feel

future forward available then upon interested last sales complete must per additional best insurance want request account give sure today interest check find report course because further here what

might return good possible since let percent take amount mail due every day/complete course/people need/special interest/just under last month/return check/upon request/sales price/good opportunity

gwam 1' | 1 | 2 | 3 | 4 | 5 | 6 | 7 | 8 | 9 | 10 | 11 | 12 | 13 |

Drill 10 continued on next page.

TIMED

Timed Writings
(3'- and 5'-timed writings continued)

---

104. WHAT IS A RESUME?   *gwam* 3'

A resume is a brief account of the qualifications of an ap- 4 | 50
plicant for a position. A resume frequently accompanies a letter 8 | 55
of application or an employment application. An accurate and 12 | 59
well-devised resume is one of the best methods to make a good im- 17 | 63
pression on a prospective employer. A resume may have personal 21 | 67
information, background data such as work experience and educa- 25 | 71
tion, references, and added skills related to the job. The per- 29 | 76
sons whom you list as references in a resume should have already 34 | 80
given their consent to be listed. Firms may have their own per- 38 | 84
sonnel forms to fill in, but it is often a good plan to have your 42 | 89
own resume. Always make sure that your resume is up to date. 46 | 93

gwam 3' | 1 | 2 | 3 | 4 |

---

105. RENTING OR BUYING?   *gwam* 3' | 5'

For a business, renting is a method of obtaining property 4 | 2 | 48
without a large sum of capital outlay. At the same time, some of 8 | 5 | 50
the other reasons for renting are worth exploring. Renting as- 12 | 7 | 53
sists in cutting down on a large volume of paperwork, since the 17 | 10 | 55
cost is usually paid in one lump sum on a periodic basis. By 21 | 13 | 58
renting, a firm does not have to compute depreciation or to pay 25 | 15 | 60
property taxes. In most cases, the cost of insurance is included 30 | 18 | 63
in the periodic payment. Finally, after the rental period, a 34 | 20 | 66
business does not have to dispose of the used property. 37 | 22 | 68

At other times, buying property may be a better alternative 41 | 25 | 70
to renting. Buying may supply some tax advantages and, at the 46 | 27 | 73
same time, equity frequently builds up as the payments are made. 50 | 30 | 75
Interest paid on items owned is often a tax deduction along with 54 | 33 | 78
insurance, licenses, depreciation, and other related expenses. 59 | 35 | 80
You often have more choices of what to buy compared with what can 63 | 38 | 83
be rented. At some point, the buyer will actually own the prop- 67 | 40 | 86
erty. You may find that it is best to buy some items and rent 71 | 43 | 88
others based on a given situation at the time a decision is made. 76 | 45 | 91

Timed writings continued on next page.

gwam 3' | 1 | 2 | 3 | 4 |
5' | 1 | 2 | 3 |

Drill 10
(continued)

Third 100 words

offer better high think write name advise charge full general tax
pleased card attached members period rate stock until long public
property board association note recent credit case back total few

where believe making paid regarding without important come months
contract attention national prices job week receipt federal given
payment able following reply position type therefore soon several

committee both money application employees happy copies equipment
pay system building book concerning home while receive items list
product loan free him great set hospital within invoice life less

having provide supply own customers increased personal look basis
rate paid months enclosing passed reply position while prices few
set rate/better offer/paid bill/loan payment/reply soon/high tax/

gwam 1' | 1 | 2 | 3 | 4 | 5 | 6 | 7 | 8 | 9 | 10 | 11 | 12 | 13 |

First 300 Words

Please thank your department for the program which may be of use.
An insurance policy is available upon request for your committee.
Therefore, forward our mail as I am very interested in the sales.

Return the attached course today before the first school meeting.
We appreciate the help received from each office during the year.
He might mail us a receipt for the payment on our property today.

A system to account for my material in the hospital was not sent.
Members will receive future copies with the opportunity to reply.
Our company is happy about the tax service which you can provide.

However, we need to advise you about the additional course items.
Please check the enclosed order of our customers after next week.
A credit list was given to employees by the first of every month.

gwam 1' | 1 | 2 | 3 | 4 | 5 | 6 | 7 | 8 | 9 | 10 | 11 | 12 | 13 |

Drill 10 continued on next page.

Timed Writings
(3'- and 5'-timed
writings continued)

102. APPLICATION LETTER

gwam 3'

A letter of application is frequently your first contact	4 50
with a firm in which you are seeking employment. A well-written	8 54
letter of application is one of the best ways to introduce your-	12 58
self as a prospective employee. Attempt to make the letter un-	17 62
lock the door for an interview. Thus, the letter should not have	21 67
any errors, should include a short presentation about yourself,	25 71
and should present a brief summary of what you have to offer.	29 75
Incorporate any other items that are requested in the announce-	34 79
ment of the position. Unless other instructions are given to	38 84
you, key the letter using a personal computer with a suitable	42 88
font. Be sure to print the letter on a high grade of paper.	46 92

gwam 3' | 1 | 2 | 3 | 4 |

103. MANAGEMENT STYLES

gwam 3' 5'

An autocratic management style is one approach for reaching	4 2 48
decisions regarding the major and some minor issues in a firm.	8 5 51
This management style institutes a great deal of decision making	13 8 53
and delegation of authority in the hands of one or a very few in	17 10 56
a firm. Some firms embrace this as a superior style, especially	21 13 59
when there is not a distinct channel of command. When this style	26 15 61
is used, those not in the highest level assume that policy and	30 18 64
other matters will be dictated to them. If you are not involved	34 21 66
in the decision making, this style may be perplexing to you.	38 23 69
Another management style institutes a great deal of decision	42 25 71
making in the hands of many key people. When this approach is	47 28 74
used, delegation is the rule rather than the exception to the	51 30 76
rule. This is known as a democratic management style. It pulls	55 33 79
varied persons in a firm into the decision-making process. Under	59 36 81
this style, there is a channel of command that attempts to allow	64 38 84
input from as many levels as feasible in a firm. This style is	68 41 87
very popular and has often replaced the autocratic management	72 43 89
style that was more typical of the management styles of the past.	76 46 92

Timed writings contin-
ued on next page.

gwam 3' | 1 | 2 | 3 | 4 |
5' | 1 | 2 | 3 |

SKILLBUILDING

Drill 10
(continued)

Part B
To increase your speed, key each of the four groups of drills on this and the next page.

Fourth 100 Words

go tact rates place thanks issue change probably between problems serve records did held show claim value statement right field ask another done going shown visit market required operation purchase

services too keep needs regards states letters various management continue bank men record don't glad shipment whether income group experience division staff savings recently requirements certainly

questions even four local students small reference membership why addition requested plans still member current assistance delivery problem section water government kind county education production

annual college manager companies does sending cannot contact five organization ever cooperation effective approximately change size representative president field customer operation power reference

gwam 1' | 1 | 2 | 3 | 4 | 5 | 6 | 7 | 8 | 9 | 10 | 11 | 12 | 13 |

Fifth 100 Words

care meet point subject support issued dealers balance here cover project ago ten page orders reason second trust working low forms convenience box old law sheet world premium machine large quality

notice question district oil room direct regular dated protection original always become fill end down store taken agency completed benefits never community hand said file real looking address cash

dealer effort sale costs books already planning control unit fine family weeks asked writing either desire returned defense inquiry consideration merchandise study immediately training suggest once

administration construction covering schedule advertising balance industry appreciated pleasure read development page world writing always taken looking books put individual little along meet large

gwam 1' | 1 | 2 | 3 | 4 | 5 | 6 | 7 | 8 | 9 | 10 | 11 | 12 | 13 |

Drill 10 continued on next page.

Timed Writings
(3'- and 5'-timed writings continued)

  A

100. COMPUTER GRAPHICS

gwam 3'

For many years, people thought of a graphic as a hand-drawn 　4 | 51
image or a picture on a page. Now that it is easy to obtain 　8 | 55
graphics software for the personal computer, the situation has 　12 | 59
changed. Graphics software provides a copy of an actual picture 　17 | 63
or a drawing, or it will let the user finish a drawing by the use 　21 | 68
of software tools. A photograph taken with a digital camera or 　25 | 72
some other equipment is often used as a graphic. Text is also 　30 | 76
easily added to a graphic. Different types of fonts are used for 　34 | 81
this purpose. The use of graphics provides an opportunity for a 　38 | 85
company to complete professional looking documents within the 　42 | 89
company rather than paying an outside source for graphics work. 　47 | 93

gwam 3' | 1 | 2 | 3 | 4 |

101. HARDWARE/SOFTWARE

gwam 3' | 5'

One of the first topics you will talk about in your personal 　4 | 2 | 49
computer class is the difference between computer hardware and 　8 | 5 | 51
software. Your teacher may tell you that the hardware consists 　13 | 8 | 54
of the computer itself and all of the related physical equipment 　17 | 11 | 56
that is needed for you to use the computer properly. Some of the 　21 | 13 | 59
hardware you will find out about includes disk drives, keyboards, 　26 | 15 | 61
modems, printers, and monitors. It is important that you learn 　30 | 18 | 64
how to clean and care for all of your computer hardware. You 　34 | 20 | 66
must also learn to properly turn on and off all of the equipment. 　38 | 23 | 69

You will learn in class that computer software directs the 　42 | 25 | 71
hardware to do its work in the proper way. You may already know 　47 | 28 | 74
about a common type of software, a word processor. Other kinds 　51 | 31 | 77
include database, spreadsheet, desktop publishing, and graphics. 　55 | 33 | 79
Often these are included in one integrated package that is sold 　60 | 36 | 82
at a very reasonable price. Software costs are most likely based 　64 | 38 | 84
on the quality and quantity of work that the software will allow 　68 | 41 | 87
a personal computer to do. It's very important that your hard- 　72 | 43 | 90
ware have enough memory to run the software that you want to use. 　77 | 46 | 92

Timed writings continued on next page.

gwam 3' | 1 | 2 | 3 | 4 |
5' | 1 | 2 | 3 |

SKILLBUILDING

Drill 10
(continued)

Sixth 100 Words

yet bonds item street sample perhaps needed others product unable far class areas posts thought purpose shipped below director open indicated her loss sell paper attend doing reserve student enough

including against say tell wishes you'll reports plant operations monthly furnish answer act she times found policies model average materials understand sold labor entire cases certain proposed off

receiving listed doctor bring cents convention sincerely approval telephone written discuss benefit commission action changes short result rather include helpful envelope connection executive funds

together immediate means situation provided investment trade half facilities increased personnel item agreement employment policies particular air prior street six areas expect her connection cases

gwam 1' | 1 | 2 | 3 | 4 | 5 | 6 | 7 | 8 | 9 | 10 | 11 | 12 | 13 |

Part C
Take a 2' timed writing on the paragraphs. Repeat all of Drill 10 beginning on page 12 as time permits.

First 600 Words   gwam 1' | 2'

Support of a customer is very important. A business should   12 | 6

show that customers are appreciated. With good customer support   25 | 13

a business may find an opportunity for increased sales. There-   37 | 19

fore, a business must offer products and services to meet the   50 | 25

wishes and needs of customers. Since management plays such a   62 | 31

large part in the operations of a business, it should provide an   75 | 38

opportunity for better cooperation with customers and employees.   88 | 44

Also, customers have a special interest in the consider-   11 | 50

ation given them by a business. In most cases, the customers are 24 | 56

always right when a problem develops. However, this is not al-   37 | 62

ways the case; the business may have a policy regarding certain   49 | 69

situations in which the customer may be considered wrong. Even   62 | 75

then, the business may give assistance to the customer, rather   75 | 81

than disregard the customer. This is a way to receive support   88 | 88

from a customer in providing for future growth and development.   100 | 94

gwam 1' | 1 | 2 | 3 | 4 | 5 | 6 | 7 | 8 | 9 | 10 | 11 | 12 | 13 |
     2' | 1 | 2 | 3 | 4 | 5 | 6 |

Timed Writings
(3'- and 5'-timed writings continued)

98. WHAT IS A DATABASE?

gwam 3'

A database is a collection of information arranged for ease | 4 | 50
and speed to search or retrieve. It is mainly a list with infor- | 8 | 55
mation that may be used now or in the future. Think of a data- | 12 | 59
base as a filing cabinet with different types of information that | 17 | 63
is kept for present and future use. All types of small firms and | 21 | 68
individuals use the personal computer for managing a database. | 26 | 72
Larger computers are most likely used when the volume warrants | 30 | 76
them. At times, software for a database is used without any | 34 | 80
change made to it. In some cases, software is programmed for a | 38 | 84
specific type of database used in a firm. A database allows a | 42 | 89
user to easily choose only the information required as needed. | 46 | 93

gwam 3' | 1 | 2 | 3 | 4 |

99. ELECTRONIC MAIL

gwam 3' | 5'

Electronic mail, commonly referred to as E-mail, is often | 4 | 2 | 48
used as a fast and fun way to send and receive messages. The | 8 | 5 | 50
number of E-mail messages sent and received each day is amazing. | 12 | 7 | 53
E-mail may be used for personal and business purposes. If you | 17 | 10 | 55
use an Internet connection, E-mail does not often cost extra. | 21 | 13 | 58
Since it is so fast, E-mail is a great way to ask for information | 25 | 15 | 60
you need right away. To send and receive E-mail, you must have | 30 | 18 | 63
an address. Your E-mail address, like your postal address, must | 34 | 20 | 66
be unique. Otherwise, someone else might get your messages. | 38 | 23 | 68

E-mail software is used to send and receive messages. Some | 42 | 25 | 71
software is free and may be downloaded from the Internet. There | 46 | 28 | 73
may be very little support or help for this kind of software. | 51 | 30 | 76
E-mail software is often included in the cost of an account with | 55 | 33 | 78
an Internet server, who is likely to provide good support and | 59 | 35 | 81
help for its software. E-mail software may be bought by itself. | 63 | 38 | 83
A firm that sells this software often provides good support in | 68 | 41 | 86
making sure it functions properly. With more and more practice, | 72 | 43 | 88
you will find that E-mail software is very easy to use. | 76 | 45 | 91

Timed writings continued on next page.

gwam 3' | 1 | 2 | 3 | 4 |
5' | 1 | 2 | 3 |

SKILLBUILDING

Drill 11 •
Rhythm Drills

Part A
To improve speed, key a 1'
writing on each group of three
lines.

FEATURE: Balanced-hand, one-hand, and combinations.

BENEFIT: Improve keystroking rhythm.

TECHNIQUE TIP: Key with quick, even rhythm.

GOAL: To build continuity and a smooth stroking rate.

Two- and Three-Stroke Balanced-Hand Phrases

sit or/did die/he dug/fix it/six men/key to/men own/aid me/do own
do so/by air/sit by/pen pal/bow tie/big bus/ham and/lap dog/go to
did go/but if/so she/got us/and due/so icy/the man/pan of/big bid

pro spa/go but/pay for/if it/he may/eye for/big dog/wig fit/it is
box of/go pay/apt to/an owl/the ale/rug dye/cut ivy/eye for/so it
man by/dig or/may pay/he lay/if she/dot of/big end/nap or/bus key

gwam 1' | 1 | 2 | 3 | 4 | 5 | 6 | 7 | 8 | 9 | 10 | 11 | 12 | 13 |

Part B
Key a 1' writing on each group
of three lines. Try to increase
your speed by two gwam over
Part A.

Three- and Four-Stroke Balanced-Hand Phrases

city sign/clay bowl/did halt/rich man/corn cob/big risk/make them
when may/cod fish/rush for/they work/worn sock/soap dish/big town
body form/turn down/busy men/firm fit/pay half/also sign/the lane

box with/key goal/bus duty/lake dock/bush burn/auto fuel/own both
they envy/torn gown/tick tock/half and/big rock/city map/sick pay
sit down/town spa/own name/both wish/lamb born/the sock/rich coal

gwam 1' | 1 | 2 | 3 | 4 | 5 | 6 | 7 | 8 | 9 | 10 | 11 | 12 | 13 |

Part C
Key a 1' writing on each group
of three lines. If you did not
increase your speed by two
gwam over Part A and Part B,
rekey Part C at your best rate.

Four- and Five-Stroke Balanced-Hand Phrases

they focus/firm shape/shame them/make eight/they paid/usual vigor
right hand/busy world/city audit/giant flame/panel held/turn down
spend half/giant risk/fight kept/amend panel/they laugh/firm hand

firm world/ivory fork/held tight/throw half/wish their/right fuel
their fury/sick virus/flame burn/work cycle/both visit/spent them
also visit/vivid risk/civic duty/amend both/right angle/duel lens

gwam 1' | 1 | 2 | 3 | 4 | 5 | 6 | 7 | 8 | 9 | 10 | 11 | 12 | 13 |

*Drill 11 continued on
next page.*

Timed Writings
(3'- and 5'-timed writings continued)

  A

96. SPREADSHEET SOFTWARE

gwam 3'

A spreadsheet has rows and columns of numbers. It also has	4 | 50
formulas to do various types of calculations. You can easily	8 | 54
change the formula, add data, or make corrections. If one or	12 | 58
more items are changed in a spreadsheet, new results are auto-	16 | 62
matically figured. You can create bar, pie, and line charts	20 | 66
of your data with most spreadsheet software. Because of the	25 | 70
large amount of time required and the need for accuracy, use the	29 | 75
most up-to-date software and the fastest personal computer that	33 | 79
you can afford. These types of programs are often part of a	37 | 83
larger suite of programs that may also include a database, a word	42 | 87
processor, and maybe even a program for creating presentations.	46 | 92

gwam 3' | 1 | 2 | 3 | 4 |

97. INVESTMENT GOALS

gwam 3' | 5'

Investing is a process that often requires sound research	4	2 | 48
and expert advice. People have many ways to invest. Real	8	5 | 50
estate, gold, and silver are only a few types of investments.	12	7 | 53
Stocks and bonds are very popular. A person may buy stocks and	16	10 | 55
bonds through mutual funds, or they may be bought directly.	20	12 | 58
Often people invest in pension plans. Many times these plans are	25	15 | 60
used over several years with proceeds that often start at the	29	17 | 63
time a person retires. Social security is also a popular kind of	33	20 | 65
investment. The benefits often add to a plan for retirement.	38	23 | 68
The goals of individuals often determine the different types	42	25 | 70
of investments that are made. These goals may vary during the	46	28 | 73
life of a person; thus the investments may also vary from time to	50	30 | 76
time. Frequently, people have one or two primary goals in mind	55	33 | 78
or a combination of the two. One of these goals is that of hav-	59	35 | 81
ing a secure investment. This may mean less return and probably	63	38 | 83
less increase in the value of the investment. Another goal is to	67	40 | 86
invest at a higher risk to realize a greater return, but indi-	72	43 | 88
viduals should never invest more than they can afford to lose.	76	45 | 91

Timed writings continued on next page.

gwam 3' | 1 | 2 | 3 | 4 |
         5' | 1 | 2 | 3 |

SKILLBUILDING

Drill 11
(continued)

Part D
To improve speed, key two
1' writings on each group of
three lines.

Balanced-Hand Expanded Phrases

if it did/if it did land/if it did land by/if it did land by them
the busy/the busy men/the busy men handle/the busy men handle the
go to the/go to the lake/go to the lake by/go to the lake by auto

when did/when did they/when did they visit/when did they visit us
both paid/both paid for/both paid for the/both paid for the gowns
if they/if they spend/if they spend six/if they spend six visible

gwam 1' | 1 | 2 | 3 | 4 | 5 | 6 | 7 | 8 | 9 | 10 | 11 | 12 | 13 |

Part E
Key two 1' writings on each
group of three lines. Try to
increase your speed by two
gwam over Part D.

One-Hand Expanded Phrases

my only/my only eager/my only eager pupil/my only eager pupil was
we agree/we agree on/we agree on union/we agree on union averages
read my/read my estate/read my estate deed/read my estate deed on

look at/look at my/look at my greatest/look at my greatest awards
I saw my/I saw my puppy/I saw my puppy eat/I saw my puppy eat wet
we created/we created a/we created a pink/we created a pink nylon

gwam 1' | 1 | 2 | 3 | 4 | 5 | 6 | 7 | 8 | 9 | 10 | 11 | 12 | 13 |

Part F
Key a 1' writing on each group
of three lines. If you did not
increase your speed by two
gwam over Part D and Part E,
rekey Part F at your best rate.

Combination Expanded Phrases

look for/look for cars/look for cars in/look for cars in downtown
did they/did they join/did they join the/did they join the extras
save the/save the duty/save the duty rates/save the duty rates on

we only handle/we only handle baggage/we only handle baggage upon
when you/when you fix/when you fix their/when you fix their vases
do they/do they vacate/do they vacate my/do they vacate my scarce

they saved/they saved a/they saved a seat/they saved a seat extra
do taxes/do taxes on/do taxes on audit/do taxes on audit timeline
my worn/my worn car/my worn car tested/my worn car tested visible

*Drill 11 continued on
next page.*

gwam 1' | 1 | 2 | 3 | 4 | 5 | 6 | 7 | 8 | 9 | 10 | 11 | 12 | 13 |

Timed Writings
(3'- and 5'-timed writings continued)

94. WORD PROCESSING

gwam 3'

Preparing text is very different now than in the past. For   4 | 50
example, words that were recorded at slow rates through writing   8 | 55
by hand or keying on a typewriter can now be processed at a very   13 | 59
fast rate by use of the personal computer. Various up-to-date   17 | 63
software programs for word processing are now in use with the   21 | 67
personal computer. These programs allow for very fast input and   25 | 72
checking for errors in spelling and grammar. Work with tables,   30 | 76
envelopes, and labels is made easier. A printout is made pos-   34 | 80
sible by a combination of software and a printer that results in   38 | 84
mailing quality, if desired. In our world today, the use of up-   42 | 89
to-date word processing is basic to a good communication system.   46 | 93

gwam 3' | 1 | 2 | 3 | 4 |

95. TAKE-HOME SALARY

gwam 3' | 5'

You either have had or will have a great shock when you re-   4 | 2 | 48
ceive your first take-home salary. Hopefully, you have not pre-   8 | 5 | 50
pared a budget based on your gross salary. The amount of your   12 | 7 | 53
take-home salary likely is smaller than you expected. Because   17 | 10 | 56
of certain deductions, you will discover that the gross amount of   21 | 13 | 58
your salary changes. These deductions are generally a result of   25 | 15 | 61
local, state, and federal tax laws. With greater income and   29 | 18 | 63
lower number of exemptions, the higher is the amount deducted.   34 | 20 | 66
Check for errors to make sure that the net salary is correct.   38 | 23 | 68

The exact amount that is deducted from a salary varies among   42 | 25 | 71
people. For example, the income tax for state and local purposes   46 | 28 | 73
may vary depending on your location. Usually, you can count on   50 | 30 | 76
social security tax as a deduction. Health and life insurance   55 | 33 | 78
deductions are often shared with an employer. At times, a person   59 | 35 | 81
may have money deducted on a regular basis from a credit union.   63 | 38 | 84
Also, most types of retirement plans require a large deduction   68 | 41 | 86
from your salary, which is often tax deferred. Once you retire,   72 | 43 | 89
you have to pay income tax on any of the tax-deferred proceeds.   76 | 46 | 91

Timed writings continued on next page.

gwam 3' | 1 | 2 | 3 | 4 |
5' | 1 | 2 | 3 |

Drill 11
(continued)

Part G
To improve speed, key two 1' writings on each group of three lines.

Balanced-Hand Sentences

With the right element for focus, a firm may make a giant profit.
Did she go downtown to sign the forms and the title for the auto?
She may wish to work with the social panels and the civic panels.

Do they also dig for authentic antique, ivory tusks by an island?
When did they fix the bicycle for the neighbor with the sick dog?
They wish to make the turkey dish and the fish dish for the dorm.

gwam 1' | 1 | 2 | 3 | 4 | 5 | 6 | 7 | 8 | 9 | 10 | 11 | 12 | 13 |

Part H
Key two 1' writings on each group of three lines. Try to increase your speed by two gwam over Part G.

One-Hand Sentences

You were eager after you referred my opinion poll on trade facts.
Based on a radar test, cars raced on a loop uphill at fast rates.
Get data on a set effect in aggravated stress cases my crew gave.

Extra minimum fees were added on after I reassessed estate taxes.
Are you aware we tasted yummy deserts after we tasted my cabbage?
Career staff referred him as average degree grades were affected.

gwam 1' | 1 | 2 | 3 | 4 | 5 | 6 | 7 | 8 | 9 | 10 | 11 | 12 | 13 |

Part I
Key a 1' writing on each group of three lines. If you did not increase your speed by two gwam over Part G and Part H, rekey Part I at your best rate.

Combination Sentences

The six firms wish to make the monopoly in the world trade areas.
The union is eager to set key goals to decrease their added work.
Jo agreed to focus on a theme after we set a date for the social.

Their tax firm states the estate may pay a tax due on the assets.
Jim may state when the city auditor at work is at risk for debts.
Turn their water down after they soak the grease on their handle.

The car tags are due at the end of May so she reassessed in town.
Their enamel on a brass antique shelf was fusible, but also oily.
Mandy is to go in a cab to the address we stated and do the work.

Drill 11 continued on next page.

gwam 1' | 1 | 2 | 3 | 4 | 5 | 6 | 7 | 8 | 9 | 10 | 11 | 12 | 13 |

TIMED

Timed Writings
(3'- and 5'-timed writings continued)

92. EARNING A PROMOTION

gwam 3'

What do you know about promotions in the world of business?	4	51
First, promotions often take place, and they occur for varied	8	55
reasons. Second, promotions are not often automatic; rather they	13	59
must be earned by hard and honest work for a firm. Third, pro-	17	63
motions very often result in an increase in salary, a change in	21	67
title, and a different series of tasks on a job. Fourth, promo-	25	72
tions are often earned by persons who project good knowledge and	30	76
skills as employees on the job. Fifth, promotions may require	34	80
moving to other geographic locations. In summary, there is much	38	85
to know about promotions, but knowing a great deal about a job	42	89
and having good working skills are key to getting a promotion.	46	93

gwam 3' | 1 | 2 | 3 | 4 |

93. LISTENING TO MUSIC

gwam 3' | 5'

What kinds of music do you prefer to listen to? It appears	4	2	48
that every era has its own style of music. You might prefer more	8	5	50
than one kind of music and even dislike other kinds. Your indi-	13	8	53
vidual taste might well determine the kinds of music that you	17	10	55
like or dislike. There is loud music, soft music, or music in	21	13	58
between. To a great extent, individuals tend to prefer music	25	15	60
that they heard when they were young. You often find that others	30	18	63
also prefer your favorite kinds of music. However, you probably	34	20	66
have certain music scores that are your personal favorites.	38	23	68
There are varied ways of listening to music. Television and	42	25	71
radio are popular, as are various devices for listening to re-	46	28	73
corded music. A concert by a group or an individual seems popu-	50	30	75
lar almost all of the time. Taking part in some type of musical	54	33	78
group also helps you both hear and enjoy music. As we listen to	59	35	81
music, we might marvel at the professional musician who through	63	38	83
years of hard work can create music that will live for a long pe-	67	40	86
riod. Surely, life would be less enjoyable if we did not have a	72	43	88
chance to experience listening to our favorite kind of music.	76	45	91

*Timed writings contin-
ued on next page.*

gwam 3'
5'

Drill 11
(continued)

Part J
To improve speed, key a 1'
writing on each of the paragraphs. Key a 2' writing on
the three paragraphs.

Balanced-Hand Paragraph

gwam 1' | 2'

Firms may make a profit when chaotic work problems stop. | 12 | 6
Problems of a firm may cause it to take risks for a visible prof- | 24 | 12
it. To rid firms of problems, goals might shape patterns to in- | 37 | 19
crease profit with little or no decrease in the quantity of work. | 50 | 25

One-Hand Paragraph

gwam 1' | 2'

My staff agreed to look up data based on average grades of | 12 | 31
a pupil in the first year at school. After locating data on the | 25 | 37
pupil, my staff set up an opinion poll. Extra pupils were asked | 38 | 44
if only average grades were affected by added stress on them. | 50 | 50

Combination Paragraph

gwam 1' | 2'

A mode of travel is by air. The rate of travel is a stated | 12 | 56
goal when certain people travel by air. However, problems are | 25 | 62
known to occur at various times with baggage. Radar has averted | 38 | 69
many problems with air travel plus added up-to-date aircraft. | 50 | 75

gwam 1' | 1 | 2 | 3 | 4 | 5 | 6 | 7 | 8 | 9 | 10 | 11 | 12 | 13 |
2' | 1 | 2 | 3 | 4 | 5 | 6 |

Part K
To improve speed, key a 2'
writing on the three paragraphs. Try to increase your
speed by two gwam over the
2' writing in Part J. Repeat
Part K as time permits, trying
to increase your speed by two
gwam.

Balanced-Hand, One-Hand, Combination Paragraphs

gwam 1' | 2'

If an amendment to the city bill is voted for, the city | 11 | 6
panel may need to form a new theme. The panel may fight to amend | 24 | 12
rigid, antique bills. A social for the panel is scheduled for | 37 | 19
next week to dispel any haughty views that may not be right. | 49 | 25

We debated a fact that taxes decreased on estate acreage. | 12 | 30
A minimum fee is now set each year for taxes on estate acreage. | 25 | 37
For taxes to decrease, join in a debate to defeat the rate in | 37 | 43
effect and create a better tax rate on acreage and estates. | 50 | 49

When you start to work, you may focus on only a few career | 12 | 55
choices. As you search for a career, you can refer to certain | 24 | 61
professionals for their opinions. It is very common to search | 37 | 68
for the quality individual to establish the career objectives. | 49 | 74

gwam 1' | 1 | 2 | 3 | 4 | 5 | 6 | 7 | 8 | 9 | 10 | 11 | 12 | 13 |
2' | 1 | 2 | 3 | 4 | 5 | 6 |

TIMED

Timed Writings
(3'- and 5'-timed writings continued)

     A

90. WHAT IS A MORTGAGE?

gwam 3'

	3'
A mortgage is a legal document that confirms the conditions	4 51
under which certain kinds of property may be repossessed if pay-	8 55
ments are not made. Interest is often charged on mortgages. A	13 59
very common mortgage is a mortgage on the residence in which a	17 63
family lives. Payments are often made each month on a long-term	21 68
mortgage until it is paid off in full. The mortgage is then re-	25 72
leased and the property is free of the mortgage. Mortgages of a	30 76
similar nature are utilized in the world of business. Short-term	34 81
loans are also common for personal and business reasons. Mort-	38 85
gages are often required for these loans. A penalty is often not	43 89
assessed for the early payment of short- or long-term loans.	47 93

gwam 3' | 1 | 2 | 3 | 4 |

91. FAST FOOD FRANCHISES

gwam 3' | 5'

	3'	5'
Some of your favorite places to eat may be stores with the	4	2 47
reputation that they can provide food to you quickly. These	8	5 50
firms more than likely maintain the same standards regardless of	12	7 52
location. In many cases, these fast food places are located next	17	10 55
to or near each other. They are very often located on well-	21	12 58
traveled highways and streets. Often they are franchises that	25	15 60
are a part of a larger number of companies. As these firms work	29	18 63
toward a high volume of sales, these franchises try to provide	34	20 65
the same menus and other items from one location to another.	38	23 68
Firms that are franchised and are known for their fast food	42	25 70
service often hire a large number of part-time employees. These	46	28 73
employees often start at or near a minimum wage without most of	50	30 75
the employee benefits that are often extended to the full-time	54	33 78
employees. Buying of food and supplies in large quantities cuts	59	35 80
expenditures, and these savings are often passed on to the con-	63	38 83
sumer. Advertising on the national level is then a joint en-	67	40 85
deavor with other firms in the same franchise. As you can easily	71	43 88
observe, a firm benefits in many ways by being a franchise.	75	45 90

Timed writings continued on next page.

gwam 3' | 1 | 2 | 3 | 4 |
5' | 1 | 2 | 3 |

SKILLBUILDING

Drill 12 •
Two-Minute
Goal Writings

1. If your goal is speed, strive to key the entire paragraph in two minutes. If your goal is accuracy, attempt to key the paragraph in two minutes with two errors or less.

2. Select an appropriate paragraph depending upon your goal.

3. Key the next longer paragraph if you meet your goal.

Note: One-minute writings begin on page 25.

FEATURE: Eighteen 2' goal writings from 20-54 words a minute. Each writing increases by two words a minute.

BENEFIT: Increase speed or accuracy by keying toward specific goals.

TECHNIQUE TIP: Attempt to reach either your speed or accuracy goal, but not both at the same time.

GOAL: To increase speed or accuracy.

Goal Writing 1: 20 gwam
gwam 2'

In ancient times, people traveled mainly by walking. Those	6
people who wanted to travel had very little hope of conquering	12
any distance. Handmade sleds drawn by animals were used to move	19
large items.	20

gwam 2' | 1 | 2 | 3 | 4 | 5 | 6 |

Goal Writing 2: 22 gwam
gwam 2'

Later in history, people took to riding on the backs of	6
animals as a mode of travel. Camels, oxen, and donkeys preceded	12
horses for travel in early times. Not until later did horses	18
become the main animals used for travel.	22

gwam 2' | 1 | 2 | 3 | 4 | 5 | 6 |

Goal Writing 3: 24 gwam
gwam 2'

A significant travel advancement in early times was the in-	6
vention of the wheel. Because of the conditions of roads and	12
lack of roads, the wheel had little effect on travel for years.	19
The first wheel was mainly used with carts and wagons.	24

gwam 2' | 1 | 2 | 3 | 4 | 5 | 6 |

Goal Writing 4: 26 gwam
gwam 2'

Travel by boat evolved as the use of the wheel and of pack	6
animals became more common. Larger boats could carry more people	13
and items than most animals and simple carts. Canoes, rafts, and	19
galleys with square sails were used for travel, trading, and	25
warfare.	26

Drill 12 continued on next page.

gwam 2' | 1 | 2 | 3 | 4 | 5 | 6 |

Timed Writings
(3'- and 5'-timed writings continued)

88. OWNER OR EMPLOYEE?

gwam 3'

As you consider a future in business think about these ques- 4 | 50
tions: First, would you aspire to own your own business someday? 8 | 54
Second, would you prefer the status of an employee, where you 13 | 59
will work for someone else? Also, you need to know that failure 17 | 63
rates are high for new businesses and that finding working capi- 21 | 67
tal is often a big challenge. Although the risk may be higher 25 | 71
for a business owner, the monetary gains and rewards may be much 30 | 76
greater than for an employee. If you work full-time for a busi- 34 | 80
ness you will gain some benefits, such as insurance. After com- 38 | 84
pleting a large amount of research, you will be able to decide 42 | 88
between owning your own business or becoming an employee. 46 | 92

gwam 3' | 1 | 2 | 3 | 4 |

89. COMPETITION AND YOU

gwam 3' | 5'

Most individuals have competed in a class activity or a 4 | 2 | 47
sporting event. During a class, competition often develops when 8 | 5 | 50
you are ranked with others in some type of activity. During a 12 | 7 | 52
game in a sporting event, competition occurs between individuals 17 | 10 | 55
or teams. As you compete, the way you respond to others often 21 | 13 | 57
shows much about you as a person. Whether your team wins or 25 | 15 | 60
loses, the response you give to your own members and to those on 29 | 18 | 62
the other side should be positive. If you compete in a sporting 34 | 20 | 65
event as an individual, this type of attitude is also needed. 38 | 23 | 67

One of the most common types of competition involves com- 41 | 25 | 70
peting with yourself. You should attempt to do your best at all 46 | 27 | 72
times so that once the competition is completed, you can honestly 50 | 30 | 75
believe that you gave your best whether you performed as an 54 | 32 | 77
individual or as a member of a team. Competing with yourself can 59 | 35 | 80
assist you in determining how much you are improving from one 63 | 38 | 82
period of time to the next. Although it is exciting to be a win- 67 | 40 | 85
ner, it is often more rewarding to hear someone say that you dem- 71 | 43 | 88
onstrated your best ability while the game was played. 75 | 45 | 90

Timed writings continued on next page.

gwam 3' / 5'

Drill 12
(continued)

Goal Writing 5: 28 gwam

gwam 2'

Most early travel devices relied on natural resources to	6
generate the power for movement. Human and animal strength,	12
wind, and water currents propelled vehicles over land and water.	18
Fuel was first used efficiently to power travel when Robert	24
Fulton invented the steamboat in 1807.	28

gwam 2' | 1 | 2 | 3 | 4 | 5 | 6 |

Goal Writing 6: 30 gwam

gwam 2'

The railroad is a mode of travel that is still used today.	6
One of the earliest railroads consisted of horse-drawn cars on	12
wooden rails. Soon horses were replaced with steam power. Today	19
we rely on the railroad to transport goods of all sorts across	25
the country. Passenger travel is also available.	30

gwam 2' | 1 | 2 | 3 | 4 | 5 | 6 |

Goal Writing 7: 32 gwam

gwam 2'

The development of the super highway system has taken	5
decades. Roads have improved gradually throughout the country--	12
progressing from single paths, to roughly paved roads, to the	18
vast interstate system we have today. The interstate system is	24
used heavily by the trucking industry and by leisure and business	31
travelers.	32

gwam 2' | 1 | 2 | 3 | 4 | 5 | 6 |

Goal Writing 8: 34 gwam

gwam 2'

Travel for most people comes in various styles and forms.	6
Many people rely on public transportation such as passenger	12
trains and buses. Other people own some type of vehicle for	18
travel. Every year the automobile industry introduces new models	25
that have improvements over earlier models. Thus, some people	31
buy a new car every few years.	34

Drill 12 continued on next page.

gwam 2' | 1 | 2 | 3 | 4 | 5 | 6 |

Timed Writings
(3'- and 5'-timed writings continued)

  A

86. BUSINESS AND THE LAW

gwam 3'

Sound legal advice is often sought by firms. Firms that do	4 | 50
not consider legal counsel primary to their welfare may have a	8 | 54
great deal of trouble. Legal problems for a firm can occur in-	12 | 58
side and outside its walls. Hiring personnel and the directing	17 | 62
of regular employees are only two inside areas where legal ad-	21 | 66
vice is needed. Relations with clients and others who have con-	25 | 70
tact with a firm represent outside areas that may also invite	29 | 75
legal actions. If it can, a firm must have access to the best	33 | 79
legal counsel. Some firms have their legal counsel on a re-	37 | 83
tainer. It is important that firms prevent legal problems before	42 | 87
they happen rather than try to solve them after they happen.	46 | 91

gwam 3' | 1   2   3   4 |

87. TRAVELING MODES

gwam 3' | 5'

Three primary modes of traveling are by land, on water, and	4 | 2 | 48
in air. Each of these has unique advantages and disadvantages.	8 | 5 | 51
Air is the fastest of the three ways of travel. If you want to	13 | 8 | 53
save money, you might travel by land. Land travel is especially	17 | 10 | 56
economical when several people ride in one vehicle. To travel in	21 | 13 | 58
luxury, people often choose to travel on water in cruise ships.	26 | 15 | 61
To plan travel in advance is always desirable. However, at times	30 | 18 | 64
an emergency requires that plans must be made immediately. In	34 | 21 | 66
any case, select the mode of travel that best meets your needs.	39 | 23 | 69
People travel for both personal and professional reasons.	42 | 25 | 71
Most personal travel consists of short trips from your home to a	47 | 28 | 74
nearby location. Traveling for a vacation is considered to be	51 | 31 | 76
personal travel. Vacations are often long and require overnight	55 | 33 | 79
lodging. The mode of business travel chosen often varies based	60 | 36 | 81
on the time needed to leave and to arrive. The ease and the cost	64 | 38 | 84
are considered before someone makes a trip for business. If time	68 | 41 | 87
is a main factor, air may be your best choice. Use of an auto	73 | 44 | 89
often saves money when several stops occur on a trip.	76 | 46 | 91

Timed writings continued on next page.

gwam 3' | 1   2   3   4 |
      5' | 1   2   3 |

Drill 12
(continued)

Goal Writing 9: 36 gwam

gwam 2'

People generally own autos for several purposes. First, car | 6
owners may desire to simply drive for pleasure and recreation. | 13
Second, car owners may require an auto to drive to and from work | 19
or utilize them for business travel on the job. Third, the own- | 25
ners may need the auto for both purposes. In any case, autos | 32
need good maintenance for maximum performance. | 36

gwam 2' | 1 | 2 | 3 | 4 | 5 | 6 |

Goal Writing 10: 38 gwam

gwam 2'

Our world seems much smaller now that worldwide travel and | 6
communication are easily available. Satellites placed in orbit | 12
with spaceships bring to us the news as it is actually occurring | 19
in a foreign land. Air travel is becoming commonplace as air- | 25
ports expand service to most cities. Advances in cable and | 31
computer technology bring us the Internet's speed and sophis- | 37
tication. | 38

gwam 2' | 1 | 2 | 3 | 4 | 5 | 6 |

Goal Writing 11: 40 gwam

gwam 2'

As more people in our nation retire, traveling as a hobby | 6
should become more popular. Retirees can choose from domestic or | 12
foreign cruises and tours. Travel to countries in eastern Europe | 19
and southeast Asia is now readily available through most travel | 25
agencies. For drivers, good fuel prices and more efficient autos | 32
make road travel appealing and a good value. Air travel should | 38
continue to grow. | 40

gwam 2' | 1 | 2 | 3 | 4 | 5 | 6 |

Goal Writing 12: 42 gwam

gwam 2'

The fastest mode of travel available for us is by air. Air | 6
travel has increased each year with coast-to-coast trips not at | 12
all unusual. There is also an increase in the number of regional | 19
airports that connect directly to larger cities. With the advent | 26
of larger and faster airplanes that can travel longer distances | 32
without refueling, air travel to foreign lands is popular. A | 38
trend for more air travel is expected. | 42

Drill 12 continued on next page.

gwam 2' | 1 | 2 | 3 | 4 | 5 | 6 |

A

84. ACCOUNTING ON COMPUTERS
gwam 3'

The personal computer is often used to record, summarize,	4 | 51
and analyze accounting data for a firm. The size of a firm and	8 | 55
the type and number of transactions often dictate the require-	12 | 59
ments for the personal computer and software that are used. For	17 | 63
example, in smaller firms one computer is often used for all of	21 | 68
the input and output of data. In larger firms a network system	25 | 72
is often used. This system allows two or more personal computers	30 | 76
to be linked together for the input and output of data. Because	34 | 81
of the need for unique accounting functions, software is at times	38 | 85
programmed for specific use by a firm. In other cases, some type	43 | 89
of generic accounting software is purchased for use by a firm.	47 | 94

gwam 3' | 1 | 2 | 3 | 4 |

85. YOUR INSURANCE NEEDS
gwam 3' \| 5'

Why do you think insurance is needed? First, it is a tool	4 | 2 | 48
to reduce losses as a result of specific happenings that are not	8 | 5 | 51
presently anticipated. Some examples are loss of life, health	13 | 8 | 53
problems, fire, hail, floods, and auto accidents. Second, insur-	17 | 10 | 56
ance is a tool to provide financial security. You need to think	21 | 13 | 58
of only one major disaster to discern that financial security	25 | 15 | 61
might be lost without insurance. Third, insurance allows you to	30 | 18 | 63
have peace of mind. To know that you are able to replace or at	34 | 20 | 66
least partially replace a potential loss gives peace of mind.	38 | 23 | 68
Insurance takes many forms. The many types of insurance	42 | 25 | 71
available may confuse a person or a family seeking coverage. It	46 | 28 | 73
is a good idea to talk with other people you trust to find out	50 | 30 | 76
what kinds of insurance they have. Reliable and honest agents	54 | 33 | 78
from varied insurance firms may also be of great help. Shop for	59 | 35 | 81
insurance just as you shop for other kinds of goods and services.	63 | 38 | 83
Health, property, and life insurance are some main kinds of in-	67 | 40 | 86
surance that need attention. Although families may differ in the	72 | 43 | 89
amount of coverage, everyone needs certain kinds of insurance.	76 | 46 | 91

*Timed writings contin-
ued on next page.*

gwam 3' | 1 | 2 | 3 | 4 |
5' | 1 | 2 | 3 |

Drill 12
(continued)

Goal Writing 13: 44 gwam

gwam 2'

Land travel is very popular with many people.   The most com- 6
mon modes of land travel are by autos and trucks.   Autos are used 13
widely for both personal travel and business travel.   Newer fea- 19
tures on autos are making it safer for individuals who use these 25
vehicles.   Trucks with added safety features often provide travel 32
for business and industry in our country.   In either case, super 38
highways are providing a boost to this type of travel. 44

gwam 2' | 1 | 2 | 3 | 4 | 5 | 6 |

Goal Writing 14: 46 gwam

gwam 2'

An outgrowth of air travel is travel into space.   From the 6
first spaceship that landed in the ocean to the space shuttle 12
that lands conventionally, hard work and many dollars have gone 19
into these programs.   The space shuttle is utilized over and over 25
again for varied purposes.   There is also a space station for use 32
in outer space.   Some pioneers have walked on the moon, while 38
others have lost their lives.   There is a great future for air 44
travel into space. 46

gwam 2' | 1 | 2 | 3 | 4 | 5 | 6 |

Goal Writing 15: 48 gwam

gwam 2'

There can be no doubt that travel has changed in many ways 6
from even fifty years ago.   People can travel almost anywhere in 12
the world by land, sea, and air.   A second change is the ease of 19
arranging for the various modes used for personal travel and 25
business travel.   A third change is the increased usage of 31
private and public transportation for commuting from home to 37
work.   A fourth change is the ability of persons to travel very 43
quickly from one location to another location. 48

gwam 2' | 1 | 2 | 3 | 4 | 5 | 6 |

*Drill 12 continued on
next page.*

TIMED

82. VALUING FRIENDSHIPS

gwam 3'

One of your goals should be to strive to be liked and not to	4 | 50
be disliked. This means that you must treat others as you would	8 | 55
like them to treat you. Even though this attempt does not guar-	13 | 59
antee success in developing friendships, it greatly increases	17 | 63
your chances to find rewarding relationships. If you genuinely	21 | 67
desire to like others with whom you associate, the results are	25 | 71
often very effective. You need to value those you care about and	30 | 76
endeavor to give to others as well as to receive from others.	34 | 80
You should not assume that friendships occur without efforts on	38 | 84
your part. You need to nurture friendships. A friendship nur-	42 | 88
tured over a long period will often remain over the years.	46 | 92

gwam 3' | 1 | 2 | 3 | 4 |

83. LAW ENFORCEMENT

gwam 3' | 5'

Why do we need law enforcement in our society? When you	4	2 | 47
really think about this question, you do not arrive at any simple	8	5 | 50
answers. We often think first of some crime that has been com-	12	7 | 52
mitted that requires action by the police. This is only one	16	10 | 55
small phase of law enforcement. In a broader sense, almost any-	21	12 | 57
thing we do and say has some bearing on the law. Thus, we should	25	15 | 60
perceive law enforcement as essential for an orderly society. It	29	18 | 63
should also foster fairness to all persons in our society. Think	34	20 | 65
about the alternatives in our nation without law enforcement.	38	23 | 68
Law enforcement takes different forms. In addition to pro-	42	25 | 70
tection from crime, law enforcement may assist in the personal	46	28 | 73
and business aspects of your life. For example, if you assume	50	30 | 76
that you have a case, you have the privilege to take your diffi-	54	33 | 78
culty to a small claims court or even much higher. If you do	59	35 | 80
require legal aid, you may need to secure competent counsel to	63	38 | 83
establish your part, if any, in an incident that could involve	67	40 | 85
the law. Thus, you have the right to a system of law enforce-	71	43 | 88
ment that attempts to protect you in varied legal situations.	75	45 | 90

Timed writings continued on next page.

gwam 3' | 1 | 2 | 3 | 4 |
5' | 1 | 2 | 3 |

Drill 12
(continued)

Goal Writing 16: 50 gwam

gwam 2'

A mode of travel that is often overlooked is the type that   6

requires only the power of an individual. The most popular type   12

of travel vehicles of this nature is the bicycle. It is used in   19

our country for personal and business purposes. Persons will   25

often ride a bicycle for exercise. Others will use it for riding   32

to school or to work. There are persons who like to ride on bi-   38

cycles for long distances as a hobby. Varied persons use the   44

bicycle for making deliveries and patrolling the streets.   50

gwam 2' | 1 | 2 | 3 | 4 | 5 | 6 |

Goal Writing 17: 52 gwam

gwam 2'

One major concern that affects the mode of travel a person   6

chooses is the cost involved. When a small group can travel in   12

one auto and time is not a great factor, this is probably the   19

cheapest means of traveling. If time is a factor on long trips,   25

more than one driver is often used without stopping overnight.   31

Therefore, the cost of lodging on the trip does not occur. Buses   38

and trains in some geographic areas of our nation have good   44

service and economic prices. Air travel is the most expensive,   50

but the fastest.   52

gwam 2' | 1 | 2 | 3 | 4 | 5 | 6 |

Goal Writing 18: 54 gwam

gwam 2'

Another mode of travel that is often overlooked is by water.   6

This is one of the oldest modes of travel in history. Travel for   13

personal and business uses occurs both inland and in the ocean.   19

Cruise ships are frequently chosen by individuals who travel to   26

islands or other vacation resorts located on or near the ocean.   32

Large and small barges carry all manner of goods over long and   39

short distances. Travel by water may be somewhat slower than   45

other major modes of travel, but it is generally more economical   51

and can support larger loads.   54

gwam 2' | 1 | 2 | 3 | 4 | 5 | 6 |

TIMED

80. MONEY AND YOUR LIFE

gwam 3'

A common way to define money is that it is a medium of	4 | 50
exchange. Although money is very significant, there are indi-	8 | 54
viduals who insist that money is the most essential element in	12 | 58
their lives. Do you reject this belief? Would you rather have a	16 | 62
healthy body and a sound mind than to have money? Would you	20 | 66
rather have good friends and those who care for you than to save	25 | 71
money? Would you rather be respected and admired by others than	29 | 75
to spend money? Your reaction to these and related questions de-	33 | 79
notes your value system. This does not mean that you cannot have	38 | 84
a suitable balance. Once you attain the desirable balance in	42 | 88
your value system, hopefully you will properly use your money.	46 | 92

gwam 3' | 1 | 2 | 3 | 4 |

81. PAYING YOUR TAXES

gwam 3' | 5'

Several distinct taxes exist. One primary tax is the income	4	2 | 48
tax. This tax is levied on the national level and frequently by	8	5 | 50
states and lower levels of government. The income tax is a prog-	13	8 | 53
ressive tax because the rates increase as adjusted gross income	17	10 | 55
of the taxpayer increases. The sales tax is frequently levied on	21	13 | 58
state and local levels but not at the national level. The sales	26	15 | 61
tax is a proportional tax because the rates do not normally fluc-	30	18 | 63
tuate on totals of sales. For persons who are at a low income	34	21 | 66
level, the proportional tax is considered regressive in nature.	38	23 | 68
Why do we pay taxes? Taxes are paid for varied reasons.	42	25 | 71
Money to operate agencies of the government is secured with	46	28 | 73
taxes. Taxes often provide funds for education. Further, taxes	51	30 | 76
protect us against crime. Highways are funded by the use of	55	33 | 78
taxes. The national forests and many of our lakes are often	59	35 | 80
taken care of with the collection of tax money. You may wisely	63	38 | 83
choose to define taxes as a way of sharing. Although we alone	67	40 | 86
cannot provide the many services desired by society, this is	71	43 | 88
often feasible by sharing our money through taxes with others.	75	45 | 91

Timed writings continued on next page.

gwam 3' | 1 | 2 | 3 | 4 |
      5' | 1 | 2 | 3 |

Section B One-Minute Progressive Writings

FEATURE: Twenty-one 1' progressive writings from 20-60 words a minute. Each writing increases by two words a minute.

BENEFIT: Success motivates.

TECHNIQUE TIP: Practice for either speed or accuracy.

GOAL: To complete the writing within one minute (speed goal) or to complete the writing within one minute with one error or less (accuracy goal).

PROGRESSIVE

1. Select a paragraph, based on the speed of your keying.

2. Key for one minute. Drive to complete the timing.

3. Repeat the timing until you can key it without errors.

4. Progress to the next paragraph if you meet your goal.

Note: Additional progressive writings begin on page 83.

20 gwam
gwam 1'

    A hobby is an activity or interest pursued outside a regular   12
occupation, done chiefly for amusement.   20

gwam 1' | 1 | 2 | 3 | 4 | 5 | 6 | 7 | 8 | 9 | 10 | 11 | 12 | 13 |

22 gwam
gwam 1'

    At times a hobby might become a major business endeavor of   12
an individual with the hobby. This is one outcome.   22

gwam 1' | 1 | 2 | 3 | 4 | 5 | 6 | 7 | 8 | 9 | 10 | 11 | 12 | 13 |

24 gwam
gwam 1'

    Most people have at least one hobby in which they show an   12
interest. The hobbies vary from one person to another person.   24

gwam 1' | 1 | 2 | 3 | 4 | 5 | 6 | 7 | 8 | 9 | 10 | 11 | 12 | 13 |

26 gwam
gwam 1'

    Jogging is a type of exercise or hobby. A person may jog   12
during various times in a day. Early morning hours are often   24
preferred.   20

gwam 1' | 1 | 2 | 3 | 4 | 5 | 6 | 7 | 8 | 9 | 10 | 11 | 12 | 13 |

28 gwam
gwam 1'

    A popular hobby is collecting insects. This hobby often   11
starts at an early age. In some instances, this hobby starts at   24
school or at play.   28

gwam 1' | 1 | 2 | 3 | 4 | 5 | 6 | 7 | 8 | 9 | 10 | 11 | 12 | 13 |

30 gwam
gwam 1'

    A widespread outdoor hobby is fishing. An individual can   12
often enjoy fishing in lakes, in ponds, and in streams. Another   25
good place is in the ocean.   30

gwam 1' | 1 | 2 | 3 | 4 | 5 | 6 | 7 | 8 | 9 | 10 | 11 | 12 | 13 |

Progressive writings continued on next page.

TIMED

Timed Writings
(3'- and 5'-timed
writings continued)

78. MUTUAL FUNDS AND YOU *gwam 3'*

Mutual funds are very popular in our society today. Mutual   4 | 50
funds provide an effective way to invest for income and capital   8 | 55
growth. As you invest in a mutual fund, you purchase shares of   13 | 59
the fund. The number of shares you own depends on the amount   17 | 63
you invest and on the price of each share. These funds help to   21 | 67
bring together the money of many people for investing the money   25 | 72
in stocks, bonds, and other types of securities. Before invest-   30 | 76
ing in mutual funds, you must establish your financial goals.   34 | 80
How much risk you are willing to take and how many years you have   38 | 84
to invest are two very important considerations. Of course, you   42 | 89
should research fully a mutual fund before investing in it.   46 | 93

gwam 3' | 1 | 2 | 3 | 4 |

79. REDUCING POLLUTION *gwam 3' | 5'*

Pollution is taking place each moment, making our natural   4 | 2 | 48
resources more impure and unclean. Some of the worst problems   8 | 5 | 50
facing not only our nation but also other nations are those of   12 | 7 | 53
pollution. In some cases, a case of pollution is not apparent   17 | 10 | 55
to us until there is some type of disaster. At other times,   21 | 12 | 58
a problem is readily seen even before it occurs. In either case,   25 | 15 | 60
much hard work must be done by experts to make sure we have a   29 | 17 | 63
safe environment for our population. We can also help by learn-   33 | 20 | 65
ing about the sources of pollution and by working on solutions.   38 | 23 | 68

Why is the issue of pollution so serious? One of the major   42 | 25 | 70
reasons why pollution is so serious is that life itself is   45 | 27 | 73
quickly affected. For example, the air we breathe and the water   50 | 30 | 75
we drink are essential to life and are harmed by pollution. Many   54 | 33 | 78
volunteer organizations work to reduce pollution and increase the   59 | 35 | 80
awareness of its threat to our lives. Although funds are needed   63 | 38 | 83
to secure more safety measures to reduce pollution, we must seek   67 | 40 | 86
new ways of dealing with it. We must be sure that through our   71 | 43 | 88
actions we help solve the problem and do not contribute to it.   76 | 45 | 91

Timed writings continued on next page.

gwam 3'
5' | 1 | 2 | 3 | 4 |
| 1 | 2 | 3 |

Progressive Writings
(continued)

32 gwam

gwam 1'

A hobby chosen by many individuals is watching movies. The   12
widespread use of devices for watching movies at home has helped   25
to increase interest in this hobby.   32

gwam 1' | 1 | 2 | 3 | 4 | 5 | 6 | 7 | 8 | 9 | 10 | 11 | 12 | 13 |

34 gwam

gwam 1'

Some hobbies take place in the outdoors. Camping is a major   12
one. Other hobbies frequently take place while you are camping.   25
For instance, you may fish, canoe, or hike.   34

gwam 1' | 1 | 2 | 3 | 4 | 5 | 6 | 7 | 8 | 9 | 10 | 11 | 12 | 13 |

36 gwam

gwam 1'

Gardening outdoors and indoors is a rewarding hobby. When   12
a person gardens outdoors, it is not year round. However, hobby   25
greenhouse kits provide for affordable indoor gardening.   36

gwam 1' | 1 | 2 | 3 | 4 | 5 | 6 | 7 | 8 | 9 | 10 | 11 | 12 | 13 |

38 gwam

gwam 1'

A relaxing hobby is reading. This includes a very broad   11
range of reading material. An example of current and short-term   24
reading is a newspaper. An example of long-term reading is a   37
novel.   38

gwam 1' | 1 | 2 | 3 | 4 | 5 | 6 | 7 | 8 | 9 | 10 | 11 | 12 | 13 |

40 gwam

gwam 1'

A hobby that might appeal to you is team sports. This type   12
of sport is often a game. Competition of a team is an important   25
aspect. However, you may enjoy team sports without any formal   37
competition.   40

gwam 1' | 1 | 2 | 3 | 4 | 5 | 6 | 7 | 8 | 9 | 10 | 11 | 12 | 13 |

42 gwam

gwam 1'

Photography is frequently a hobby or a career. Persons may   12
own their own studio. People may also enjoy taking photos of   24
family, friends, and scenery. An amateur may even win a prize   37
in a photography contest.   42

Progressive writings continued on next page.

gwam 1' | 1 | 2 | 3 | 4 | 5 | 6 | 7 | 8 | 9 | 10 | 11 | 12 | 13 |

TIMED

Timed Writings
*(3'- and 5'-timed
writings continued)*

76. ANNUITY INVESTMENTS

gwam 3'

	3'
If you invest in an annuity, income for a certain number of	4	50
years or over your lifetime is guaranteed. You may purchase an	8	54
annuity during the years that you work. In some cases, you may	13	59
purchase one at retirement age for a lump-sum payment. As no	17	63
death benefits are provided, a physical exam is not needed at	21	67
the time you buy one. You buy an annuity to supplement social	25	71
security and other types of pension plans. You may buy one that	29	75
is fixed or variable. Fixed annuities are often invested in	33	79
bonds and mortgages; a variable annuity is often invested in com-	38	84
mon stocks. You may wish to buy an annuity with both types of	42	88
investments in an effort to protect income against inflation.	46	92

gwam 3' | 1 | 2 | 3 | 4 |

77. READING OR WATCHING TV?

gwam 3' | 5'

	3'	5'
Is reading more useful than watching television? As you re-	4	2	48
late to your own situation, the answer depends on a number of	8	5	50
factors. When reading a book or attempting to locate an answer	12	7	53
to a question in a magazine, you will find information that you	17	10	55
can refer back to, if needed. At varied times you can often get	21	13	58
bits of news from news programs on television, but you will find	25	15	60
that more vital detail is often provided in a newspaper. If you	30	18	63
are attempting to research a subject in detail, television may	34	20	66
not cover it at all. Use the Internet as a viable alternative.	38	23	68
When is watching television more helpful than reading? To	42	25	70
watch television within limits provides information in a way	46	28	73
similar to reading. Television brings world events to you at a	50	30	75
quicker pace than is the case with a book or magazine. But you	55	33	78
may find some special parts of the events are missing in tele-	59	35	80
vision programs. You may then need to read in order to examine	63	38	83
the fine details. However, both reading about and watching a	67	40	85
television program on a subject can give more meaning. They sup-	71	43	88
port each other in various ways and are very important tools.	75	45	90

*Timed writings contin-
ued on next page.*

gwam 3' 5'

PROGRESSIVE

Progressive Writings
(continued)

44 gwam   *gwam* 1'

Traveling is a hobby for most people. Some persons like to   12
travel and may select careers that allow them to travel. Others   25
plan their own vacations every year. Some vacations are close to   38
home and others are far away.   44

gwam 1' | 1 | 2 | 3 | 4 | 5 | 6 | 7 | 8 | 9 | 10 | 11 | 12 | 13 |

46 gwam   *gwam* 1'

A relaxing hobby is watching sports on television. When   11
persons do not wish to take part in sports, they can enjoy sports   24
on television. Coverage of sports on television allows persons   37
to watch regional and international sports.   46

gwam 1' | 1 | 2 | 3 | 4 | 5 | 6 | 7 | 8 | 9 | 10 | 11 | 12 | 13 |

48 gwam   *gwam* 1'

Because swimming is great exercise, it is one of the more   12
popular hobbies. It is the type of hobby that is done strictly   24
for fun or for skill development for formal team and individual   37
competition. It is either an outdoor or indoor hobby.   48

gwam 1' | 1 | 2 | 3 | 4 | 5 | 6 | 7 | 8 | 9 | 10 | 11 | 12 | 13 |

50 gwam   *gwam* 1'

Listening to music is a hobby for certain persons. Creating   12
music is often both a hobby and a profession. Playing one or   25
more musical instruments is another type of hobby. Your musical   38
talent may open several doors for you and bring joy to others.   50

gwam 1' | 1 | 2 | 3 | 4 | 5 | 6 | 7 | 8 | 9 | 10 | 11 | 12 | 13 |

52 gwam   *gwam* 1'

The use of metal detectors is a hobby that does not often   12
provide important findings. However, the fun of looking for what   25
may be found is often exciting. Someone with a metal detector   37
must know the places to avoid and the places where detectors may   50
be used.   52

Progressive writings continued on next page.

gwam 1' | 1 | 2 | 3 | 4 | 5 | 6 | 7 | 8 | 9 | 10 | 11 | 12 | 13 |

Timed Writings
(3'- and 5'-timed writings continued)

  A

74. MAKING DECISIONS
gwam 3'

Do you like or dislike making decisions on a regular basis?	4 | 51
Whether you readily want to admit it, you are a decision maker.	8 | 55
The types of decisions you will make vary in terms of their mag-	13 | 59
nitude. Magnitude is determined by the nature of the decision	17 | 63
and by how many people the decision might affect. Further, you	21 | 68
are a decision maker even when you have to deal with decisions	25 | 72
made by others. If you like to make decisions, you may be inter-	30 | 76
ested in a management position. If not, you may choose another	34 | 81
level and serve as a receiver who carries out certain decisions.	38 | 85
You are often both a decision maker and a decision receiver. You	43 | 89
must learn to cope well with either one of these positions.	47 | 93

gwam 3' | 1 | 2 | 3 | 4 |

75. YOUR CREDIT UNION
gwam 3' \| 5'

Employees often take advantage of the services offered by	4 | 2 | 47
credit unions in their firms. A credit union is often used by an	8 | 5 | 50
employee who wants to borrow, invest, or save. In some ways, a	13 | 8 | 53
credit union has services similar to a small bank or savings and	17 | 10 | 55
loan association. However, a credit union is owned by its em-	21 | 13 | 58
ployees. Credit unions differ from most banks in that they do	25 | 15 | 60
not offer as many services. Also, credit unions, which stress	29 | 18 | 63
short-term loans to consumers, differ from savings and loan as-	34 | 20 | 65
sociations, which stress long-term loans on real estate.	37 | 22 | 67
Credit unions often have lower overhead costs than firms	41 | 25 | 70
that offer short-term loans and savings accounts. As a result of	45 | 27 | 72
lower costs and the ease of receiving payments, interest on loans	50 | 30 | 75
is often lower than those of other kinds of firms having these	54 | 32 | 77
types of services. Also, the interest paid on savings is often	58 | 35 | 80
higher. An employee is often allowed to have a set amount with-	63 | 38 | 83
held from payroll checks to collect on loans or to receive as	67 | 40 | 85
savings. To protect the employee, a credit union has the same	71 | 43 | 88
governmental insurance plans on funds deposited as other firms.	75 | 45 | 90

Timed writings continued on next page.

gwam 3' | 1 | 2 | 3 | 4 |
5' | 1 | 2 | 3 |

Progressive Writings
(continued)

54 gwam

gwam 1'

Hobbies are often seasonal sports. Water skiing is mainly a 12
summer sport, while snow skiing is most often popular during the 25
winter. Some other sports are also popular. Several of these 38
sports often overlap into more than one season. A team game 50
sport is an example. 54

gwam 1' | 1 | 2 | 3 | 4 | 5 | 6 | 7 | 8 | 9 | 10 | 11 | 12 | 13 |

56 gwam

gwam 1'

Fixing items or doing odd jobs may begin as a hobby. The 12
hobby might include working on old automobiles or fixing broken 24
items around the house. However, there are examples of persons 37
who find they have a knack for fixing things, which may lead to 50
full- or part-time employment. 56

gwam 1' | 1 | 2 | 3 | 4 | 5 | 6 | 7 | 8 | 9 | 10 | 11 | 12 | 13 |

58 gwam

gwam 1'

A popular hobby is the use of varied types of remote control 12
devices. For example, small model airplanes are often flown by 25
remote control with maneuvers very similar to regular airplanes. 38
Small model vehicles such as trains, trucks, and cars are also 51
commonly operated by remote control. 58

gwam 1' | 1 | 2 | 3 | 4 | 5 | 6 | 7 | 8 | 9 | 10 | 11 | 12 | 13 |

60 gwam

gwam 1'

Tennis and golf are two hobbies in which persons often take 12
part. Tennis and golf are often played as a profession. Tennis 25
is a competitive game between two or four individuals. Golf is 38
enjoyed by persons of various ages. Two main types of golf are 51
played; namely, miniature golf or regular golf. 60

gwam 1' | 1 | 2 | 3 | 4 | 5 | 6 | 7 | 8 | 9 | 10 | 11 | 12 | 13 |

Timed Writings
(3'- and 5'-timed writings continued)

72. A WORKING WARDROBE

gwam 3'

Unless you get a job where standard uniforms are worn by all	4	50
employees, you need to be concerned about what you should wear to	9	55
work. As a new employee, you can copy the way that other em-	13	59
ployees dress. Unless your position is very unique, you probably	17	63
already have adequate clothing for your first week of work. As	21	67
you buy new work clothing, keep within the general standards of	25	72
your firm. How can you keep your work wardrobe up to date as	30	76
styles in clothing change? Buy a few simple pieces of classic,	34	80
durable, and machine-washable clothing. You can update your	38	84
wardrobe slowly by purchasing less expensive ties, belts, and	42	88
scarves. Be sure to press and repair your clothing as needed.	46	92

gwam 3' | 1 | 2 | 3 | 4 |

73. AN EXERCISE PROGRAM

gwam 3' | 5'

Exercise is an activity that is used to develop or maintain	4	2	48
fitness. Exercise can take many forms. A person often exercises	8	5	50
on or off the job without really thinking about it. The purpose	13	8	53
of more formal exercise is to simply achieve fitness. It is	17	10	55
often practiced in a school or in a medical setting in which some	21	13	58
kinds of physical therapy are provided. In either case, the in-	25	15	60
structor has been trained to assure that the proper exercise is	30	18	63
practiced. Before any formal exercise is begun, most people work	34	20	66
with their instructor to plan out their progress and goals.	38	23	68
In too many cases, people practice a number of exercises	42	25	70
without a tried program, a thought-out plan, or the aid of a	46	28	72
trained person. These people may find they may pull muscles and	50	30	75
do their bodies more harm than they do good. Their muscles that	55	33	78
are not exercised often and on a routine basis become very sore.	59	35	80
To stop this from occurring, people should have exams from their	63	38	83
doctors and follow a program prescribed by professionals. A	67	40	86
well-rounded exercise program formed under the direction of a	72	43	88
professional is the plan that provides the best results.	75	45	90

Timed writings continued on next page.

gwam 3' | 5'

Two-Minute, Three-Minute, Five-Minute Timed Writings

Section C contains timed writings that are triple-controlled at the easy and average levels. (See page iii of the Preface for a description of triple-controlled timed writings.) Easy level timed writings are marked *E*; the average level is marked *A*. Gross words a minute (gwam) is computed automatically when you use *MicroPace Pro*. (See page iv of the Preface for information for using *MicroPace Pro*.) If you do not use *MicroPace Pro*, you may compute your gwam on your own: Add the gwam number at the end of the last completed line and the gwam at the bottom of the timed writing for a line not finished.

TIMED

Two-Minute Timed Writings

1. Do not key the title of the timed writings.

2. Follow instructions in your *MicroPace Pro* program. If you do not use *MicroPace*, use 1" margins and a .05" paragraph indent. Double-space.

3. If you finish before the time set, start over on the same timed writing.

1. PREPARE TO KEY		*gwam* 2'
When you key a job, proper use of time is vital. When time	6	63
to prepare is not managed very well, time needed to do a job	12	69
using the keyboard quite often is lost. For example, time may	18	75
be lost if you have a problem simply starting up the computer.	25	82
Realize that before you start to key, you should have handy and	31	88
in working order all of the items you need for the job. These	38	95
include your hard copy, paper, and printer. While in the process	44	101
of keying, concentrate on what you key and keep your eyes on the	51	108
copy. The rule is to prepare before you key, not as you key.	57	114

gwam 2' | 1 | 2 | 3 | 4 | 5 | 6 |

2. KEYING POSITION		*gwam* 2'
Every time you start to key, you need to take the proper	6	62
position at the keyboard. Put both feet flat on the floor and	12	68
sit with good posture. To help make it easier for you to key, be	19	75
sure to relax your arms. Keep your forearms level or just below	25	81
the top of the keyboard. At the same time, keep your wrists low	31	87
with your hands even with the slant of the keyboard. Keep your	38	94
fingers in a curved and an upright position. Place the copy on	44	100
your work area so that it is easy for you to read. Before you	51	107
key, clear items that you do not need from your work area.	56	112

gwam 2' | 1 | 2 | 3 | 4 | 5 | 6 |

3. KEYBOARD LAYOUT		*gwam* 2'
The letters are at the lower part of the keyboard. To the	6	63
right of the letters are some of the most used types of punctu-	12	69
ation. The numbers are at the top of the keyboard. Some symbols	19	76
and types of punctuation are also at the top. The shift is often	25	81
used with these keys. A ten-key pad is often on the right side	32	88
of the keyboard. Special keys are on the left side and right	38	94
side of the letters. Some of these are the tab, shift, insert,	44	100
page up, page down, and arrows. As you key, you'll find that the	51	107
fingers of the left hand work more than those of the right hand.	57	113

Timed writings continued on next page.

gwam 2' | 1 | 2 | 3 | 4 | 5 | 6 |

TIMED

Timed Writings
(3'- and 5'-timed writings continued)

70. SELECTING A CAREER   *gwam* 3'

When you consider future opportunities, you may tend to pick	4 / 51
diverse career paths. This is good because all people do not at-	8 / 56
tempt to reach out for the same opportunities. First, you might	13 / 60
want to think about your interests--your personal feelings toward	17 / 64
opportunities open to you. Second, you might want to think about	22 / 69
your aptitude--what you have the ability to do. If you consider	26 / 73
these two areas carefully and find a career that really does suit	30 / 77
you, you may increase your chances for a happy work life. How-	34 / 82
ever, as you gain more work experience and as your personal life	39 / 86
changes, you may need to reconsider your choice of a career.	43 / 90
Many people change careers at least once during their lifetime.	47 / 94

gwam 3' | 1 | 2 | 3 | 4 |

71. BORROWING MONEY   *gwam* 3' | 5'

Once you have borrowed, a debt is established that must be	4 / 2 / 48
repaid. Principal is the amount owed on a debt. Interest is the	8 / 5 / 50
amount that you pay on a debt for borrowing. You may borrow from	13 / 8 / 53
banks, small finance companies, credit unions, and other varied	17 / 10 / 56
sources. When payments are made on credit card purchases, inter-	21 / 13 / 58
est is typically paid on the unpaid balance each month. You need	26 / 15 / 61
to try to find the lowest interest rate. The law requires the	30 / 18 / 63
one from whom you borrow to indicate the actual interest rate	34 / 20 / 66
that is charged. Thus, you should know the cost of borrowing.	38 / 23 / 68
On what basis can a person borrow? You are limited on how	42 / 25 / 71
much you can borrow by differing factors, such as character, ca-	46 / 28 / 73
pacity, and collateral. Character is defined by how good your	51 / 30 / 76
reputation is and how honest you are in paying back your other	55 / 33 / 78
debts. Capacity is the ability to earn enough money to pay the	59 / 35 / 81
principal and the interest when they are due. Collateral is what	63 / 38 / 83
you own that may have to stand good for the amount borrowed.	68 / 41 / 86
Whatever your status, do not borrow unless you have ways and	72 / 43 / 88
means for repaying the amount of principal and interest owed.	76 / 45 / 91

*Timed writings contin-
ued on next page.*

gwam 3' | 1 | 2 | 3 | 4 |
      5' | 1 | 2 | 3 |

Timed Writings
(2' timed writings continued)

4. USE THE ENTER KEY

gwam 2'

The enter key is used very often. You do not use this key	6	64
to end each line. It is used most often to key at the end of a	12	70
paragraph and to space down the page. When you use it, your	18	76
right little finger will do the work. You reach and strike the	25	83
key at a fast rate and let it go. Then move back to the home-key	31	89
position at a fast rate. Do this in one motion from the original	38	96
position of your right little finger to the enter key and back to	45	103
the same position with little, if any, of your other fingers mov-	51	109
ing. Proper use of the enter key is an easy process to practice.	58	116

gwam 2' | 1 | 2 | 3 | 4 | 5 | 6 |

5. SETTING MARGINS

gwam 2'

In working with the personal computer, you will find that	6	62
margins are very easy to set and change. Margins let you control	12	68
how much white space is left along the edges of the text on a	19	75
page. Margins are set at default values--the points on a page	25	81
where you will most often need the margins set. Once these val-	31	87
ues are set, you can change the margins with very little effort.	38	94
You are able to change left, right, top, or bottom margins when	44	100
you start a page. You may wish to change margins other than at	51	107
the start of a page. This, too, is a very simple process.	56	112

gwam 2' | 1 | 2 | 3 | 4 | 5 | 6 |

6. KEYING MADE EASIER

gwam 2'

There are several ways to make keying easier. One way is to	6	64
always start with your fingers above the home-key position. An-	12	70
other way is to use a fast motion and to move quickly from one	19	77
key to the next. To help make the work of keying very simple, do	25	83
not stop and think about which is the next key. This means that	32	90
you must have proper hand position and know right away where each	38	96
of the keys is found on the keyboard. You key at your best when	45	103
you think in terms of common words or phrases. Think letter by	51	109
letter only if the words are too difficult to break into parts.	58	116

Timed writings continued on next page.

gwam 2' | 1 | 2 | 3 | 4 | 5 | 6 |

Timed Writings
*(3'- and 5'-timed
writings continued)*

    A

68. BUYING AN AUTOMOBILE

gwam 3'

The wheel, possibly the best invention of ancient times, 4 | 50
changed civilization. Of course, many modern people, young and 8 | 54
old, enjoy the four-wheeled automobile. Most people desire to 12 | 58
buy a car as soon as they have earned their driver's license. 17 | 62
However, it's not a good idea to buy the very first car that you 21 | 67
can afford. The new driver needs to think about all of the ad- 25 | 71
ditional costs of owning a car, including repairs, gas, and in- 29 | 75
surance. Once you know you can afford a car, you should talk to 33 | 79
owners, read about cars, and compare various ones before you buy 38 | 84
one. Consumer magazines offer unbiased information regarding 42 | 88
the cost, safety, and reliability of both new and used cars. 46 | 92

gwam 3' | 1 | 2 | 3 | 4 |

69. SPORTS PARTICIPATION

gwam 3' | 5'

Sports started many years ago in ancient cultures. Walls of 4 | 2 | 49
caves and other locations during those years show that some of 8 | 5 | 51
the most common sports were the high jump, the long jump, use of 13 | 8 | 54
the bow and arrow, tug of war, racing of animals, swimming, and 17 | 10 | 56
running. These and other types of sports were sometimes partici- 21 | 13 | 59
pated in before large groups of people. Most of these sports had 26 | 15 | 61
basic rules, referees, uniforms for the players, and recognition 30 | 18 | 64
for the individuals who were able to win. Beginning now at home 34 | 21 | 67
or in school, enthusiasts spend years learning to play sports. 38 | 23 | 69

Although several of the modern sports today were started in 42 | 25 | 71
ancient times, much has changed. For example, there were often 47 | 28 | 74
small rewards for those who participated in sports during ancient 51 | 31 | 77
times. The rewards for winners were often various types of col- 55 | 33 | 79
lars. Today, a person may secure a career in one or more sports 60 | 36 | 82
with very high income. With the ease of long-distance travel and 64 | 38 | 84
with increased television coverage of sporting events, the world 68 | 41 | 87
of sports is changing. However, people still have an intense 72 | 43 | 90
desire to win in several events that have stood the test of time. 77 | 46 | 92

*Timed writings contin-
ued on next page.*

gwam 3' 5' | 1 | 2 | 3 | 4 |

Timed Writings
(2' timed writings continued)

7. USE THE TEN-KEY PAD

gwam 2'

The personal computer often has a ten-key pad. It is on the | 6 | 64
right side of the keyboard. If you are working with a series of | 13 | 71
numbers, the ten-key pad is often helpful to you. When it is not | 19 | 77
used, you must reach to the top of the keyboard for each of the | 26 | 84
numbers. In some cases, this may take more time and cause more | 32 | 90
errors than using the ten-key pad. The ten-key pad may have some | 39 | 97
special keys built in. Some of these are page up, page down, in- | 45 | 103
sert, home, and end. Often the shift key is used with these spe- | 51 | 109
cial keys. Learn to use the touch system with the ten-key pad. | 58 | 116

gwam 2' | 1 | 2 | 3 | 4 | 5 | 6 |

8. HORIZONTAL SPACING

gwam 2'

You often need to space horizontally when you use the key- | 6 | 63
board. Your right thumb needs to rest almost on or very close to | 12 | 69
the space bar at all times. If the thumb puts too much pressure | 19 | 76
on the space bar, the cursor will move too quickly to the right. | 25 | 82
Always space very quickly with a down-and-in action of the right | 32 | 89
thumb. You also need to release the right thumb very quickly | 38 | 95
after the space bar is used. This means that you do not delay | 44 | 101
before or after you space. Make sure the rest of your hand does | 51 | 108
not move. You need to keep your fingers in home-key position. | 57 | 114

gwam 2' | 1 | 2 | 3 | 4 | 5 | 6 |

9. FIXED/VARIABLE RHYTHM

gwam 2'

You only have to key a few words to know that most copy is | 6 | 62
not keyed at a fixed rhythm. The point is that most copy will | 12 | 68
cause your speed to change from one word to another because of | 19 | 75
the nature of the word or group of words that are keyed. This | 25 | 81
means that your overall rate will not change much from one writ- | 31 | 87
ing to another. It means that you should not hesitate as you | 37 | 93
key. As this timed writing is on the easy level, your rhythm | 44 | 100
should be more fixed and less variable. Whatever the type of | 50 | 106
copy, key continuously both at a fixed and at a variable rate. | 56 | 112

Timed writings continued on next page.

gwam 2' | 1 | 2 | 3 | 4 | 5 | 6 |

Three-Minute and Five-Minute Timed Writings

Section C contains timed writings that are triple-controlled at the average level. All timed writings can be used with *MicroPace Pro*. (See page iv of the Preface for information about *MicroPace Pro*.)

TIMED

Three-Minute and
Five-Minute
Timed Writings

  A

66. TRAVELING IN SPACE

gwam 3'

How would you like to awake tomorrow morning and observe the	4	51
earth in its splendor from the window of a vehicle in space? In	8	55
the future, you may be able to purchase a round-trip ticket for	13	59
an excursion into space. Although the cost of the ticket would	17	63
most likely be expensive, the knowledge and skills needed to make	21	68
a trip into space for someone other than a trained astronaut is	26	72
no longer a milestone that was once presumed impossible. This	30	76
opportunity is an outcome of heroic pioneering by various persons	34	81
in our space program. Several persons have lost their lives when	39	85
serving in our space program. We should express our appreciation	43	89
to those who have pioneered our program into space.	46	93

gwam 3' | 1 | 2 | 3 | 4 |

67. CASHLESS SOCIETY

gwam 3' | 5'

Today, many financial transactions are carried on with very	4	2	47
little actual paper money passing through hands. Yet in some	8	5	49
cases, a small amount of cash may be needed. This is why most	12	7	52
people keep readily accessible a small amount in currency and	17	10	54
coins for buying minor items. Further, businesses often keep a	21	12	57
petty cash fund to take care of less expensive items. Yet, as	25	15	60
varied electronic devices become more available, the need for	29	17	62
cash-in-hand is cut back. With such devices, the security of	33	20	64
funds on line is less of a problem now than in the past.	37	22	67
Checks, telephones, automatic teller machines, personal com-	41	24	69
puters, and credit cards are only some of the major means for	45	27	72
transferring cash from one person to another. As more of these	49	30	74
devices are used, the use of electronic cash transfers will in-	53	32	77
crease. Can you believe that most people in the future will	58	35	79
make all major cash transfers from their homes? To transfer	62	37	81
these funds from home is one more example of how we are moving to	66	40	84
a cashless society that will not require the use of currency.	70	42	87
Easy-to-use software makes such transfers even more feasible.	74	45	89

gwam 3' | 1 | 2 | 3 | 4 |
5' | 1 | 2 | 3 |

Timed writings continued on next page.

Timed Writings
(2' timed writings continued)

10. KEY CORRECTLY NOW
gwam 2'

Are you an individual who keyed from the beginning with one	6	63
or two fingers of each hand? Hopefully, you were not. In any	12	69
case, individuals who keyed incorrectly at first often looked at	19	75
the keyboard while keying. If an individual keys incorrectly	25	81
over a long period, bad habits are formed that are very hard to	31	87
remedy. Ideally, you have used the touch system from the begin-	38	94
ning, making the proper key reaches and always keeping your eyes	44	100
on the copy. However, making a change to the keying process is	51	107
never too late. Start using the touch system properly right now.	57	113

gwam 2' | 1 | 2 | 3 | 4 | 5 | 6 |

11. SELECTING DRILLS
gwam 2'

Drills are often used to assist with special needs that you	6	62
have in keying. You should always know the purpose of a drill	12	68
before you key it. The best drills to select for practice help	19	75
you improve the specific key reaches that tend to slow down your	25	81
keying. Special software can help find your problem areas and	32	88
prescribe the drills that should help you the most. For example,	38	94
you may need to practice certain letter keys. Or you may have	44	100
trouble with various keystroke combinations. Drills that focus	51	107
on certain fingers, rows, and combinations are the best.	56	112

gwam 2' | 1 | 2 | 3 | 4 | 5 | 6 |

12. SHIFTING TECHNIQUE
gwam 2'

Shifting is a process most frequently used to key capital	6	63
letters and symbols. The little fingers are needed in shifting.	12	69
The right-hand shift is needed for a left-hand character, while	19	76
the left-hand shift is needed for a right-hand character. Press	25	82
down on the shift with the appropriate little finger. Strike,	32	89
almost at the very same moment, the key that you are shifting.	38	95
Release the little finger very quickly. Each step is very signi-	44	101
ficant in the process. If you need more practice, be sure to se-	51	108
lect special drills that will reinforce the steps of shifting.	57	114

Timed writings continued on next page.

gwam 2' | 1 | 2 | 3 | 4 | 5 | 6 |

Progressive Writings
(continued)

92 gwam

    Antique furniture may be bought as an investment. To have   12
success a collector must know what makes an old piece of fur-   24
niture valuable. This knowledge is usually secured by studying   37
guide books and working with other collectors. Know the fair   49
price. With a large purchase, a trusted expert is often worth   61
the cost of an appraisal. All furniture is classified by pe-   74
riods and styles. Older furniture without tool marks and screws   87
is often the most valuable.   92

gwam 1' | 1 | 2 | 3 | 4 | 5 | 6 | 7 | 8 | 9 | 10 | 11 | 12 | 13 |

94 gwam

    Photos, like oil paintings, are popular as items to collect.   12
Photos that are collected range from older silvered copper plates   26
to tintype and paper images. Photographs taken by famous photo-   38
graphers frequently bring a large amount of money. It is amazing   51
how rapidly photographs, especially the silvered copper plates,   64
have increased in value over a short period of time. As for most   77
items that are collected, guide books are available to assist   90
in collecting photos.   94

gwam 1' | 1 | 2 | 3 | 4 | 5 | 6 | 7 | 8 | 9 | 10 | 11 | 12 | 13 |

96 gwam

    Collecting jewelry may be very tricky. It is possible to   12
make jewelry appear real to the eye, but the jewelry may be arti-   24
ficial. The gems in a piece of jewelry are very important. Some   38
familiar gems include opals, diamonds, emeralds, ivory, rubies,   50
and pearls. Pure gold, which never rusts or fades, is frequently   64
mixed with another metal for use in jewelry. Gold must be la-   76
beled by karat to indicate how pure it is. Consider what appeals   89
to you when starting a collection.   96

gwam 1' | 1 | 2 | 3 | 4 | 5 | 6 | 7 | 8 | 9 | 10 | 11 | 12 | 13 |

Timed Writings
(2' *timed writings
continued*)

13. FORMATTING DOCUMENTS

gwam 2'

Formatting means to arrange, place, and space copy based on	6	63
what is standard practice for different kinds of documents. Some	13	70
of the popular documents that you are most likely to format are	19	76
memos, letters, reports, announcements, and tables. To format in	26	83
the proper way, you should follow some standard document rules.	32	89
Most of these rules concern side and top margins, line spacing,	39	96
headings, and size of a page. A firm often has its own rules for	45	102
formatting. If you know the common types of document formats,	51	107
you should be able to adapt them to any firm's formats.	57	113

gwam 2' | 1 | 2 | 3 | 4 | 5 | 6 |

14. KEYING TECHNIQUES

gwam 2'

It is certainly not by accident that you demonstrate proper	6	63
techniques when you key. To insure that your work improves with	13	70
practice, you need a genuine desire to practice the appropriate	19	76
way every time you key. First, fingers must do the work with a	25	82
direct, fast action in a curved, upright position. Second, the	32	89
hands must be positioned to incorporate little, if any, motion.	38	96
Third, fingers must be positioned over the home keys with the	44	102
thumb very lightly on or almost on the space bar. Fourth, eyes	51	109
must be kept on the copy without moving to and from the keyboard.	57	115

gwam 2' | 1 | 2 | 3 | 4 | 5 | 6 |

15. TRANSFER YOUR SKILLS

gwam 2'

When you key, the best way to transfer your skills is to key	6	63
activities that are very similar to those encountered on the job.	13	70
For example, the keying of writings under time does not demon-	19	76
strate high transfer to business letters. Thus, some kinds of	25	82
keying activities in class are not meant to prepare you directly	32	89
for specific tasks. However, these activities are needed for	38	96
other reasons. To key letters in a class is seemingly the very	44	102
best method to transfer your letter keying skills to the job.	51	109
Only a school-to-work program may provide better letter practice.	57	115

*Timed writings continued
on next page.*

gwam 2' | 1 | 2 | 3 | 4 | 5 | 6 |

Progressive Writings
(continued)

86 gwam

Glass items may be collected for fun and profit. Glass 11
collectors need to make careful purchases for several reasons. 24
First, glass is very easy to fake. Second, glass is easy to 36
break and requires careful handling. Third, good research is 49
needed to determine what glass items are most valuable now and 61
possibly in the future. Fourth, there are many different types 74
and grades of glass; some types may be difficult to identify. 86

gwam 1' | 1 | 2 | 3 | 4 | 5 | 6 | 7 | 8 | 9 | 10 | 11 | 12 | 13 |

88 gwam

If you like to collect metal items, there is a wide variety 12
of choices. As metal is an alloy (two or more elements chemi- 24
cally combined), there is not a metal object that is pure within 37
itself. For example, silver without anything added has the tex- 50
ture of oatmeal. Add a touch of copper to this silver and you 62
have a very strong alloy of sterling silver. Collectible items 75
may be made of other alloys such as pewter, bronze, and brass. 88

gwam 1' | 1 | 2 | 3 | 4 | 5 | 6 | 7 | 8 | 9 | 10 | 11 | 12 | 13 |

90 gwam

If you have visited a flea market recently, you may have 11
wondered why there are so many kitchen utensils. Most of these 24
utensils have value to a collector. They need to be usable, but 37
not in mint condition like many of the other collectibles. Of 50
course, do not buy utensils with rust holes or missing parts. 63
Some popular kitchen items that are collectible include rolling 75
pins, mixers, dishes, funnels, pots and pans, waffle irons, and 88
washboards. 90

Progressive writings continued on next page.

gwam 1' | 1 | 2 | 3 | 4 | 5 | 6 | 7 | 8 | 9 | 10 | 11 | 12 | 13 |

Three-Minute and Five-Minute Timed Writings

16. THE PACING PROCESS

gwam 3'

Pacing may help you to increase your speed or control in	4 | 51
keying. For the best results, use a computer and a good pacing	8 | 55
program. You will need to set a base rate on your own or take	12 | 59
one or more writings to set a base rate with the program. Then	17 | 63
the base rate, also called your base accuracy rate, is set by the	21 | 68
program at two gross words a minute higher. A one-minute writing	25 | 72
is keyed at this level. You try to match your pace to that of	30 | 76
the program, which marks off the pace every fifteen seconds. As	34 | 81
you key each writing, the program records your rates and changes	38 | 85
your goal based on how you do with your speed or control. This	43 | 89
way you improve speed and control, but not both at the same time.	47 | 94

gwam 3' | 1 | 2 | 3 | 4 |

17. BUSINESS LETTERS

gwam 3' \| 5'

Business letters are one of the most common types of for-	4 | 2 | 48
mats found in the world of work. Try to think of a time when you	8 | 5 | 51
got a business letter that was written by hand with a pen or a	12 | 7 | 53
pencil. You most likely never got such a letter and likely never	17 | 10 | 56
will get such a letter. However, you will find that some per-	21 | 13 | 58
sonal letters are still written by hand, but the more formal	25 | 15 | 61
personal letters and almost all of the business letters are not.	29 | 18 | 63
The extra time that it takes to write a letter by hand is only	34 | 20 | 66
one of the many reasons why a business letter is in a keyed form.	38 | 23 | 68
If you know how to use the keyboard, you need to learn how	42 | 25 | 71
to key all of the parts of the business letter, including the	46 | 28 | 73
spacing above and below all of the parts. A business letter will	50 | 30 | 76
most often have a letterhead under which you key the date. The	55 | 33 | 78
inside address, the one to whom a letter is sent, is followed by	59 | 35 | 81
the greeting. The body of a letter with one or more paragraphs	63 | 38 | 84
is next. Some letter styles have paragraphs in the body that are	68 | 41 | 86
indented, and others do not. The closing is keyed at the end of	72 | 43 | 89
the body of a letter. The closing often has more than one part.	76 | 46 | 91

Timed writings continued on next page.

gwam 3' | 1 | 2 | 3 | 4 |
5' | 1 | 2 | 3 |

Progressive Writings
(continued)

78 gwam

Dolls have become prominent items to collect. Based on the 12
prices that auction houses often receive, dolls may be a sound 25
investment. Dolls are more valuable if they are in top condi- 37
tion and in their original boxes. You do not have to disregard 50
buying a doll missing a key part. For example, an arm or leg can 63
be restored. However, overly restored dolls can quickly decrease 76
in value. 78

gwam 1' | 1 | 2 | 3 | 4 | 5 | 6 | 7 | 8 | 9 | 10 | 11 | 12 | 13 |

80 gwam

Unlike for other collectible items, the age of a book is 11
not a major factor in the value of the book. For example, a 24
first edition of a book is more valuable than other editions. 36
In the first edition, any errors are not corrected as in other 49
editions. Hence, the first edition is considered more valuable 62
than another edition with corrected errors. Of course, the 74
condition of a book is important. 80

gwam 1' | 1 | 2 | 3 | 4 | 5 | 6 | 7 | 8 | 9 | 10 | 11 | 12 | 13 |

82 gwam

Paintings are probably the most profitable of all items that 12
are collected. Because it may potentially be valuable, care- 24
ful research is needed before buying a painting. When buying an 37
expensive painting, persons should at the minimum have a letter 50
from a reputable art dealer, have it appraised, and have names of 63
previous owners. Persons should shop before buying and under- 75
stand their taste in paintings. 82

gwam 1' | 1 | 2 | 3 | 4 | 5 | 6 | 7 | 8 | 9 | 10 | 11 | 12 | 13 |

84 gwam

Persons often collect china. A piece of china is actually 12
high-quality porcelain or ceramic ware. China is the name given 25
to the product because it was first made in that country. People 38
who are uninformed about china may end up with a reproduction or 51
a fake of the original. Therefore, a trained appraiser is often 64
helpful. Some reproductions have value. However, a forgery or 77
a fake often has very little value. 84

*Progressive writings con-
tinued on next page.*

gwam 1' | 1 | 2 | 3 | 4 | 5 | 6 | 7 | 8 | 9 | 10 | 11 | 12 | 13 |

Timed Writings
(3'- and 5'-timed writings continued)

18. KEYS FOR EDITING
gwam 3'

With the computer, the cursor and the backspace key are	4 | 50
often used to edit copy on the same line. You can also move to	8 | 54
any other place in the copy with very little effort through use	12 | 58
of the mouse or arrow keys. These tools are used to move the	16 | 62
cursor to the proper place in the copy. This process is very	21 | 67
fast and easy. If only a few spaces are edited, the backspace	25 | 71
key is most likely used. If you need to take out a whole line,	29 | 75
it is often best to use the delete key to remove the line. It is	34 | 80
also easy to use the cut feature to take out several lines of	38 | 84
copy that you do not need. When you key new copy be sure to use	42 | 88
the insert mode so that the letters move forward in the copy.	46 | 92

gwam 3' | 1 | 2 | 3 | 4 |

19. SAVE KEYING TIME
gwam 3' | 5'

Do you know that time is often lost when keying? One way to	4 | 2 | 48
save time is to make good use of the touch system. For instance,	8 | 5 | 50
to keep eyes on the copy and to have fingers in the right place	13 | 8 | 53
above the keyboard are basic in saving time. Once you take your	17 | 10 | 55
eyes off of the copy, time is lost when you try to find the right	21 | 13 | 58
place to start again. The time lost is even greater when the	26 | 15 | 61
right place is not found and the wrong copy is keyed. To key	30 | 18 | 63
with the fingers in a position not above home row causes errors.	34 | 20 | 66
Time is also lost in keying while correcting these errors.	38 | 23 | 68
Another way to save time in keying is to format in a way	42 | 25 | 70
that is quick and easy. To save time you need to set some items	46 | 28 | 73
to format before you start to key. Most of these are items that	50 | 30 | 75
you use over and over again. Thus, other changes in items to	55 | 33 | 78
format are not often needed before you start to key. Items to	59 | 35 | 80
format that are often set before you start to key are the mar-	63 | 38 | 83
gins, font, and line spacing. Once the more common items are	67 | 40 | 85
set, you may need to set others as you key. Some of these are	71 | 43 | 88
where to number pages, where to set tabs, and where to center.	75 | 45 | 90

Timed writings continued on next page.

gwam 3' | 1 | 2 | 3 | 4 |
5' | 1 | 2 | 3 |

Progressive Writings
(continued)

70 gwam

gwam 1'

Stamps are collected by young and old.   A serious collector   12
of stamps tries to find and trade stamps with high value.   Others   25
collect more for fun and are less selective.   A good place to   38
start is your own mail.   If you have an envelope with a stamp   50
already affixed to it, the entire envelope may be worth more than   63
the stamp because of the postmark.   70

gwam 1' | 1 | 2 | 3 | 4 | 5 | 6 | 7 | 8 | 9 | 10 | 11 | 12 | 13 |

72 gwam

gwam 1'

Some people like to collect autographs for the pleasure of   12
getting a rare memento.   To obtain an autograph from a celebrity   25
can really be exciting.   Autographs may be on posters, photo-   37
graphs, cards, and other paper products.   These are sometimes   49
sold at auctions or through some type of lottery.   It is impor-   62
tant to ascertain that an autograph is authentic.   72

gwam 1' | 1 | 2 | 3 | 4 | 5 | 6 | 7 | 8 | 9 | 10 | 11 | 12 | 13 |

74 gwam

gwam 1'

Some persons take great pleasure in collecting comic books.   12
Some of the common ways to collect comic books are by character,   25
title, artist, and number.   The value of comic books is often   38
determined by their rarity and their condition.   Some comic books   51
are in mint condition.   A comic book in mint condition has a flat   64
cover, bright ink, and staples centered and tight.   74

gwam 1' | 1 | 2 | 3 | 4 | 5 | 6 | 7 | 8 | 9 | 10 | 11 | 12 | 13 |

76 gwam

gwam 1'

Because clocks go back for centuries and vary greatly in   11
style and size, they are a popular item for collectors.   There-   24
fore, clocks must possess some rare feature to make them valu-   36
able as collectible items.   For instance, the fine case where the   49
works of a clock are placed can cause a clock to be valuable.   62
Some old clocks, especially grandfather clocks, are often very   74
valuable.   76

gwam 1' | 1 | 2 | 3 | 4 | 5 | 6 | 7 | 8 | 9 | 10 | 11 | 12 | 13 |

Progressive writings continued on next page.

TIMED

Timed Writings
(3'- and 5'-timed writings continued)

20. COMPOSE AS YOU KEY

gwam 3'

Have you ever thought about the time that is saved by composing at the keyboard compared to writing by hand on a sheet of paper? Words seem to flow from your fingers when you think about what you compose rather than how you strike each of the keys. Thus, the more practice you get in composing as you key, the better you become in keying your thoughts. Even if you do not key a final draft the first time, consider not only the amount of time that you save but also how easy it is to go back and correct copy. As you key, try to think the words rather than each key in the word as you compose. Start composing now at the keyboard and try to do it regularly or whenever you have a chance to.	4 | 50 8 | 55 13 | 59 17 | 63 21 | 67 25 | 71 29 | 76 34 | 80 38 | 85 42 | 89 46 | 93

gwam 3' | 1 | 2 | 3 | 4 |

21. KEYBOARDING SKILLS

gwam 3' | 5'

Basic keying is when you work to reach the levels of speed and control to get ready to key in the real world. For instance, to center, to set margins, and to set tabs are basic. Also, to key numbers and some of the most often used symbols with little effort is basic. A large part of the basic work in class is done with timed writings and drills. Each writing that you key will help you to improve speed and control. The drills also help with better speed and fewer errors based on each writing. At the basic skill level, most of the work is on how to key.	4 | 2 | 45 8 | 5 | 47 13 | 8 | 50 17 | 10 | 52 21 | 13 | 55 25 | 15 | 57 29 | 18 | 60 34 | 20 | 62 38 | 23 | 65
To learn to make a decision when you key involves professional skill--or a skill that is not basic. As you work, you will need to decide if one way of keying is better than some other way. For example, why is a certain type of font used? Some others are why certain margins are set, why certain line spacing is used, and why certain tabs are used. In each one of these cases, the way to key each item is determined before you start the work. Learn why items are keyed in a certain way.	41 | 25 | 67 45 | 27 | 69 50 | 30 | 72 54 | 32 | 74 58 | 35 | 77 62 | 37 | 80 66 | 40 | 82 70 | 42 | 84

Timed writings continued on next page.

gwam 3' | 1 | 2 | 3 | 4 |
5' | 1 | 2 | 3 |

FEATURE: Eighteen 1' progressive writings from 62-96 words a minute. Each writing increases by two words a minute.

BENEFIT: Increase speed and accuracy by increasing the keyboardist's skill goal with each writing.

TECHNIQUE TIP: Practice for either speed or accuracy.

GOAL: To complete the writing within one minute or to complete the writing within one minute with one error or less.

PROGRESSIVE

1. Select a paragraph, depending upon whether you wish to increase speed or accuracy.

2. To increase speed, attempt to complete the paragraph in one minute or less. If you want to increase accuracy, attempt to complete the paragraph in one minute or less with one error or less.

3. Progress to the next paragraph if you meet your goal.

---

62 gwam   *gwam* 1'

Many people enjoy collecting items for the sheer pleasure of   12
keeping them over a long period of time. They try to increase   25
the number of these items. In other cases, people collect items   38
to make a profit. When items are collected for a profit, there   51
is usually frequent buying, trading, or selling of items.   62

gwam 1' | 1 | 2 | 3 | 4 | 5 | 6 | 7 | 8 | 9 | 10 | 11 | 12 | 13 |

64 gwam   *gwam* 1'

Baseball cards are often bought, sold, or traded. Baseball   12
cards are often traded among friends or family members. The   24
cards are sometimes collected by the age of cards, by one or more   37
players, and by certain teams. You should regard the condition   50
of a card. Look for cards that are without creases and are not   63
torn.   64

gwam 1' | 1 | 2 | 3 | 4 | 5 | 6 | 7 | 8 | 9 | 10 | 11 | 12 | 13 |

66 gwam   *gwam* 1'

Posters have become a popular item to collect. Posters that   12
relate to the movie industry are often valuable. Certain factors   25
that determine the cost of a poster are its stars, its age, and   38
its visual appeal. How popular a film became is also a factor   51
in the value of a poster. The condition of a poster is also   63
very important.   66

gwam 1' | 1 | 2 | 3 | 4 | 5 | 6 | 7 | 8 | 9 | 10 | 11 | 12 | 13 |

68 gwam   *gwam* 1'

Coin collecting is frequently passed from one generation to   12
another. The collection of coins is often fun, interesting, and   25
profitable. The grades of coins differ greatly. Coin holders   38
and albums are often needed for the storage of coins. Since you   51
do not want to damage coins, a soft pad and a coin tray make it   63
easier to handle coins.   68

gwam 1' | 1 | 2 | 3 | 4 | 5 | 6 | 7 | 8 | 9 | 10 | 11 | 12 | 13 |

Intermediate-level progressive writings continued on next page.

Timed Writings
(3'- and 5'-timed
writings continued)

22. GROSS WORDS A MINUTE

gwam 3'

Once you complete a timed writing, you may wish to know how	4	50
to figure your gross words a minute. The process to find gross	8	55
words a minute is an easy one. You divide the total number of	13	59
keyed letters by five, which is the average letters per word.	17	63
Divide the result, which is the total words, by the total time it	21	67
took to key the words. Often the time is stated in two, three,	25	72
or five minutes based on the length of the writing. If you work	30	76
with a computer program that figures gross words a minute on	34	80
writings, you do not have to take the time in doing all of the	38	84
figuring by hand. Thus, a great amount of time is saved with	42	88
results that are ready without any figuring on your part at all.	46	93

gwam 3' | 1 | 2 | 3 | 4 |

23. PROOFING FOR ERRORS

gwam 3' | 5'

You need to practice proofing over and over again. Because	4	2	48
what you key needs to be read for errors, you should make it a	8	5	50
habit to check your work every time you key. Even a rough draft	13	8	53
needs a check for errors because it often needs to be changed	17	10	55
again before a final copy is printed. Most people agree that	21	13	58
items keyed need to be read at least two times. Read once for	25	15	60
correct content and then read again for any types of technical	29	18	63
errors. Always allow time to check your work. Do not depend on	34	20	65
spell and grammar checks to do all of the checking for you.	38	23	68
Correcting an error is done once the whole copy is proofed.	42	25	70
If you key the copy without making an error the first time, this	46	28	73
means that you have done a good job. This is not always the	50	30	75
case. You may correct an error as you key, as it is often easy	54	33	78
to know when an error is made. You should go ahead and make that	59	35	80
correction. Some word processors will correct many types of er-	63	38	83
rors as you key. In any case, always check the copy before you	67	40	85
print it. If you find an error after printing a page, you will	71	43	88
need to open the file with the copy before you print again.	75	45	90

Timed writings continued on next page.

gwam 3' | 1 | 2 | 3 | 4 |
     5' | 1 | 2 | 3 |

SKILLBUILDING

Drill 14
(continued)

Sustained Writing 5: 72–74 gwam

The hard drive is another critical part of a personal | 11 | 5

computer. The hard drive is located in the console and is pro- | 23 | 12

tected from dust and other matter that might damage it. A com- | 36 | 18

puter can have more than one hard drive or an external one. The | 49 | 24

hard drive is a device that holds the hard disk. A blinking | 61 | 31

light indicates when a hard drive is in active operation. | 72 | 36

Some people may be confused about the difference between | 11 | 42

the hard drive and the hard disk. The hard disk, located in the | 24 | 48

hard drive, is a disk with the capacity to store a massive amount | 38 | 55

of information. The size of memory of a hard drive and a hard | 50 | 61

disk indicates the capacity for storing information. They may | 63 | 68

fill quickly and often need replacing with larger ones. | 74 | 73

Sustained Writing 6: 76–78 gwam

Almost all floppy disks are three and one-half inches wide. | 12 | 6

The floppy disk stores a very small amount of information when | 25 | 12

compared to a hard drive. Floppy disks are frequently utilized | 38 | 19

to transport files from one computer to another computer. | 49 | 25

Whenever there is valuable information on the hard disk that | 62 | 31

needs to be saved, the floppy disk is easily used to make backup | 75 | 37

copies. | 76 | 38

Zip drives are very popular. Although they hold consider- | 11 | 44

ably more information than a floppy drive, they are limited in | 24 | 50

their memory. As these drives are not normally on a new per- | 36 | 56

sonal computer, they must be purchased separately. Zip disks | 48 | 62

utilized in these drives look like floppy disks, but they are | 61 | 68

thicker. Zip drives are helpful in storing games, special files, | 74 | 75

and similar items. | 78 | 77

TIMED

Timed Writings
*(3'- and 5'-timed
writings continued)*

24. KEYING FOR CONTROL

gwam 3'

If you want a final copy that does not have an error, keying	4 | 51
for control is very important. To key for control means to key	8 | 55
at a rate that is easy for you to manage for both speed and accu-	13 | 59
racy. As you key, you must be in focus to make sure that you are	17 | 64
always under control. To stay under control, you may need to	21 | 68
slow down your rate of speed for a higher level of control. Try	26 | 72
to key words and phrases rather than letter by letter. Always	30 | 76
keep your eyes on the copy and be sure to use good technique with	34 | 81
your fingers at the keyboard. Some control is not enough; you	38 | 85
must have full control at all times. If you have problems with	43 | 89
control, do more practice with the goal of control in mind.	47 | 93

gwam 3' | 1 | 2 | 3 | 4 |

25. NUMBER/SYMBOL KEYS

gwam 3' | 5'

The numbers or figures on the top part of a keyboard are not	4 | 2 | 48
easy to learn. One of the reasons is that you spent a lot of	8 | 5 | 50
time at first with the letter rows, which do seem easier. The	12 | 7 | 53
letter rows are easier since they are either on or next to the	17 | 10 | 55
home keys. Also, the numbers or figures seem harder because they	21 | 13 | 58
are not used over and over again in a sentence. However, these	25 | 15 | 61
numbers or figures should become much easier to key as you prac-	30 | 18 | 63
tice them more and more. There are some drills you can do that	34 | 20 | 66
will help you learn to key the numbers and figures with ease.	38 | 23 | 68
The symbols are often thought to be the most difficult of	42 | 25 | 70
all the keys, including the number or figure keys. Almost all of	46 | 28 | 73
the symbols are on the same keys as the numbers or figures and	50 | 30 | 76
must be used with the shift key, which may help explain why they	55 | 33 | 78
are so difficult. In any case, you must not expect to key the	59 | 35 | 81
symbols as fast as letters. As with numbers or figures, the sym-	63 | 38 | 83
bols will become easier to key with practice if this is a goal	67 | 40 | 86
you have. If you work on a job that requires you to key symbols	72 | 43 | 88
over and over again, you will learn to use them very quickly.	76 | 45 | 91

Timed writings continued on next page.

gwam 3' | 1 | 2 | 3 | 4 |
5' | 1 | 2 | 3 |

SKILLBUILDING

Drill 14
(continued)

Sustained Writing 3: 64–66 gwam

gwam 1' | 2'

The console of the personal computer holds the main computer 12 | 6
unit for processing input and output. The console may be posi- 25 | 12
tioned directly under the monitor or on either side of the key- 37 | 19
board and the monitor of a desktop computer. Many desktop com- 49 | 25
puters have mini-tower consoles. A laptop computer console is 62 | 31
built in. 64 | 32

The printer provides hard copy output of processed docu- 11 | 37
ments. Advances in printer technology have made them more com- 23 | 44
pact and reasonably priced. Two common types are ink-jet and 36 | 50
laser printers. Both types of printers serve multiple purposes 49 | 56
for users. Laser printers do cost more but provide higher qual- 61 | 62
ity text and graphics. 66 | 65

gwam 1' | 1 | 2 | 3 | 4 | 5 | 6 | 7 | 8 | 9 | 10 | 11 | 12 | 13
2' | 1 | 2 | 3 | 4 | 5 | 6

Sustained Writing 4: 68–70 gwam

gwam 1' | 2'

Most printers on the market are compatible with most per- 11 | 6
sonal computers. However, check before buying. Ink-jet printers 24 | 12
use canisters of ink and laser printers use toner cartridges. 37 | 18
Check the replacement costs of cartridges and canisters before 49 | 25
you choose a printer. They are easy to load, but used canisters 62 | 31
can really be quite messy. 68 | 34

Cables are critical hardware for the personal computer. 11 | 40
Cables connect at the back of the console and are not often easy 24 | 46
to access. A basic rule is not to plug in any cable while the 37 | 52
computer is turned on. Always plug cables into the correct 49 | 58
slots. Some of the cables are for the power cord, the keyboard, 62 | 65
the mouse, the printer, and the monitor. 70 | 69

Drill 14 continued on next page.

gwam 1' | 1 | 2 | 3 | 4 | 5 | 6 | 7 | 8 | 9 | 10 | 11 | 12 | 13
2' | 1 | 2 | 3 | 4 | 5 | 6

Timed Writings
(3'- and 5'-timed writings continued)

26. HOW TO SET TABS

gwam 3'

The tab is used often at the start of a paragraph. When	4 50
software is used to key copy, a default tab stop is most likely	8 55
to be set at every half inch. You can set a stop at any place on	13 59
the page. The process to set a stop is not hard. It is easy and	17 64
quick to move to a stop by pressing the tab key. You may also	21 68
need to move a stop or delete or create one or more new ones.	25 72
This, too, is an easy and quick process. Think of the time that	30 76
you can save when you use tabs with tables that have more than	34 80
one column. Tabs are moved less in letters because of the in-	38 85
crease in use of the block style. In block letters you start all	42 89
parts of the letter at the left margin or at the first left stop.	47 93

gwam 3' | 1 | 2 | 3 | 4 |

27. KEYING REPORTS

gwam 3' | 5'

A report is one of the most common types of documents. If	4	2 48
you are new to a firm in which reports are often keyed, you will	8	5 50
need to know what format is used for the reports of the firm.	13	8 53
The reports will often range from simple in-house reports to very	17	10 56
complex reports. A firm in which reports are keyed on a routine	21	13 58
basis will often have a manual to use as a guide. The manual	25	15 61
will often have rules for margins, spacing, and other items	29	18 63
needed to key a report for the firm. In case the firm does not	34	20 66
have a manual, the use of file copies of reports should help.	38	23 68
There are some rules for keying reports that are common to	42	25 70
most firms. Most reports start with a title that is centered at	46	28 73
the start of a report. The first page of a report often does not	50	30 76
have a page number. You cannot divide a word at the end of a	55	33 78
page. It is often a rule that at least two lines must be in a	59	35 81
paragraph at the bottom of a page. When it is possible, the	63	38 83
same rule is in effect for lines on the next page of a report.	67	40 86
Often, long quotes of four or more lines are indented in the body	71	43 88
of a report. Reports for a firm may be either bound or unbound.	76	45 91

Timed writings continued on next page.

SKILLBUILDING

Drill 14 •
Sustained Writings

1. Key two 1' writings on each paragraph; then two 2' writings on both paragraphs.

2. Try to maintain your 1' rate for two minutes.

FEATURE: Second paragraph within a timing increases by two words.

BENEFIT: Build staying power.

TECHNIQUE TIP: Keep arms and hands quiet; keep motion in the fingers.

GOAL: To increase your momentum in the second half of a 2' timing.

Sustained Writing 1: 56–58 gwam

	gwam	1'	2'

The hardware of a personal computer works with software to | 12 | 6

accomplish tasks.   Hardware generally refers to the encased com- | 24 | 12

ponents of a computer system.   The CPU, keyboard, monitor, mouse, | 38 | 19

and printer are some of the components that are part of nearly | 50 | 25

all personal computer systems. | 56 | 28

A personal computer needs software to operate the hardware. | 12 | 34

The operating system of a personal computer is the most important | 25 | 41

piece of software.   When you purchase a computer, the operating | 38 | 47

system usually comes with it.   The operating system of a compu- | 51 | 54

ter may be updated from time to time. | 58 | 57

gwam 1' | 1 | 2 | 3 | 4 | 5 | 6 | 7 | 8 | 9 | 10 | 11 | 12 | 13 |
2' | 1 | 2 | 3 | 4 | 5 | 6 |

Sustained Writing 2: 60–62 gwam

	gwam	1'	2'

A personal computer keyboard has keys with letters, numbers, | 12 | 6

symbols, punctuation marks; plus shift, caps, and tab keys.   The | 25 | 12

top row contains the function keys that access help and other | 38 | 19

software functions.   Cursor control keys and usually a numeric | 50 | 25

keypad are located to the right of most keyboards. | 60 | 30

The monitor of a personal computer has a screen like a tele- | 12 | 36

vision set.   The screen needs a display adapter located in the | 24 | 42

console of the computer to function.   A display adapter is an ex- | 37 | 49

pansion card that sends signals to the screen.   A display adapter | 50 | 55

signals how color and graphics may appear on the screen. | 62 | 61

Drill 14 continued on next page.

gwam 1' | 1 | 2 | 3 | 4 | 5 | 6 | 7 | 8 | 9 | 10 | 11 | 12 | 13 |
2' | 1 | 2 | 3 | 4 | 5 | 6 |

TIMED

28. COPY DIFFICULTY

gwam 3'

Copy is often rated on how hard it is to key by the length	4 | 51
of the words, the number of syllables, and the number of words	8 | 55
from a list of common words. When all three of these factors are	13 | 59
present at a set level, you have what is known as triple-control	17 | 64
copy. How hard the copy is has an effect on the results that you	21 | 68
may have with speed or control. For instance, the writing that	26 | 72
you are keying right now is rated as easy, which is the lowest	30 | 76
level. If you compare your work on this writing with another	34 | 81
writing, make sure that the other writing is rated as easy. If	38 | 85
you compare your speed on writings from different levels, they	42 | 89
will not make sense. So note the level before you key a writing.	47 | 93

gwam 3' | 1 | 2 | 3 | 4 |

29. KEYING ENVELOPES

gwam 3' \| 5'

If you key letters in a firm, you often deal with both mail	4 | 2 | 48
coming in and going out. For mail coming in, you must open the	8 | 5 | 50
envelope, remove the contents, check and account for items that	13 | 8 | 53
may be enclosed, stamp the time of receipt, and often send the	17 | 10 | 55
envelope and its contents to some other place in the firm. If	21 | 13 | 58
you work with mail that is going out, you need to know the postal	25 | 15 | 60
rules. A copy of an up-to-date postal guide will help you with	30 | 18 | 63
this process. Even if you work in a large firm that has a cen-	34 | 20 | 65
tral place to handle mail, it is still good to know the rules.	38 | 23 | 68
If you use a word processor that lets you key an envelope,	42 | 25 | 70
it is very easy to address. The one to whom a letter is sent is	46 | 28 | 73
the same address that is copied on the front of the envelope. If	51 | 30 | 76
your firm does not have its own address on the envelope, it is	55 | 33 | 78
easy for you to have one ready to copy. Thus, you may make and	59 | 35 | 81
keep a copy of any address for mail going out or coming in for	63 | 38 | 83
future use. You can add the envelope to the file where the out-	67 | 40 | 86
going letter is placed. It is very easy to change the format	72 | 43 | 88
of the envelope so that you may use the most common sizes.	75 | 45 | 90

Timed writings continued on next page.

gwam 3' | 1 | 2 | 3 | 4 |
5' | 1 | 2 | 3 |

Drill 13 •
Numbers and Symbols

To improve accuracy, key each group of drill lines twice.

FEATURE: Emphasizes numbers, frequently used symbols, and numbers and symbols.

BENEFIT: Keyboard mastery with number and symbol keys.

TECHNIQUE TIP: Reach to the top row with a minimum of hand movement.

GOAL: To improve fluency of numbers and frequently used symbols.

Numbers

On June 3 PLUS PX moved from 129 25th Street to 1680 47th Street.
Project No. 683940 was sent on April 25 and received on April 27.
Member ID: 3874-4602-269507 was changed to ID: 1863-9507-4780913.

The credit card 5315 1990 4382 3476 was lost on May 14 or May 15.
Flight 1829 arrives in Tulsa at 6:40 p.m. and leaves at 7:35 p.m.
Application No. 520-25-6437 and No. 190-48-3867 are now accurate.

gwam 1' | 1 | 2 | 3 | 4 | 5 | 6 | 7 | 8 | 9 | 10 | 11 | 12 | 13 |

Symbols

Enter d:\setup for the CD-ROM and a:\install for the floppy disk.
There are E-mail messages for h.flowler@bwi.net & wbrown@ame.edu.
Key footnotes (use *) for publications #68, p. 2, and #679, p. 4.

End-of-year gains of 9% ($1,186,786) were 4% less than last year.
A CD dated 1/24/99 (rate--5 1/4%) was due to Del and/or May Kise.
The discount (20%) is $240 for #2487 for their end-of-month sale.

gwam 1' | 1 | 2 | 3 | 4 | 5 | 6 | 7 | 8 | 9 | 10 | 11 | 12 | 13 |

Numbers/Symbols

P.O. #4187 showed 150 cans of paint @ $8.78 per can (2/10, n/30).
For some PC platforms use "Run" a:\setup or "Add/Remove Programs."
An annuity ($973) had deductions ($150) for a net annuity ($823).

Policy #698702 had a dividend of $812 (5%) applied on January 30.
The E-mail address of Bison & Rayhan (attorneys) is bira@jet.com.
FICA (SSA) number is 447-28-5909; the UST (IRS) ID is 37-6474610.

gwam 1' | 1 | 2 | 3 | 4 | 5 | 6 | 7 | 8 | 9 | 10 | 11 | 12 | 13 |

Timed Writings
(3'- and 5'-timed writings continued)

---

30. BUILDING SPEED
gwam 3'

Speed will vary less than control over time. In other	4	50
words, speed is often stable from day to day while control is	8	54
not. Thus, you can see gains in speed easier than you can gains	12	58
in control. To build speed with good form in your work, you must	17	63
have good posture, build proper control of keys, concentrate on	21	67
your work, use the fingers in a proper way, and keep your eyes on	25	71
the copy. These are not all of the ways to help build speed--	29	76
only some of the best ones. You need to move very fast with	33	80
various types of keying drills to help build speed, but not at	38	84
the expense of doing away with proper techniques. If you try to	42	88
increase speed to very high levels, you often decrease control.	46	92

gwam 3' | 1   2   3   4 |

---

31. COPY, CUT, AND PASTE
gwam 3' | 5'

To copy and cut text is a simple process when you use word | 4 | 2 | 48

processing software. When the copy process is used, the words | 8 | 5 | 50

that you copy will stay in the same place while they also are | 12 | 7 | 53

moved to some other place in the copy. You may cut words in much | 17 | 10 | 55

the same way. Once you cut words, they no longer remain where | 21 | 13 | 58

they were, but may be pasted in another spot in your document or | 25 | 15 | 60

removed. To copy words that you want to use in another place in | 30 | 18 | 63

the document, you first highlight them. Then move the cursor to | 34 | 20 | 66

the place where you want the copy and use the copy command. | 38 | 23 | 68

As you can copy and cut words within one document, you can | 42 | 25 | 70

also paste words to other documents. To do this, a storage area | 46 | 28 | 73

that is often known as the Clipboard is used. When you move | 50 | 30 | 75

words from one place to some other place, they will first be | 54 | 33 | 78

placed in the storage area. Your computer will do this on its | 58 | 35 | 80

own--you do not need to use a new command. When you paste words, | 63 | 38 | 83

you remove them from storage and insert them where you have | 67 | 40 | 85

placed your cursor. Keep in mind that when you cut or copy you | 71 | 43 | 88

are pasting words that were stored for a time on your Clipboard. | 75 | 45 | 90

Timed writings continued on next page.

gwam 3' | 1   2   3   4 |
5' | 1   2   3 |

Drill 12
(continued)

Twelfth 100 Words

drop route submit traffic seem wanted heard felt excess move face
floor shares step turn really pounds night calls southern reasons
contribution comes shipments desk citizens green join simple word

relations young reach certified allow paying selected that's talk
worth reasonable possibly buying double explain highly hour names
technical western request presently cause reading secure treasury

figure handled fees earnings latest groups enable response thirty
providing representatives storage learn matters filed enjoy drive
realize confident automobile numbers papers figures pages finance

manufacturers qualified potential associations nature manufacture
accordingly face session publication liability accepted amendment
secretarial described generally agencies thousands prove yes face

gwam 1' | 1 | 2 | 3 | 4 | 5 | 6 | 7 | 8 | 9 | 10 | 11 | 12 | 13 |

First 1200 Words

gwam 1' | 3'

If you completed the two parts of this book, you were able	12	4	67

If you completed the two parts of this book, you were able · 12 · 4 · 67
to practice a list of several words used when you write or key. · 25 · 8 · 72
As you completed the drill in this part, you noticed that some of · 38 · 13 · 76
the words were long and difficult. However, some of the words in · 51 · 17 · 80
each part are short and easy. The words were arranged according · 64 · 21 · 85
to how often they are used when we write or key. Words that do · 77 · 26 · 89
not appear on the list are probably long and more difficult. · 89 · 30 · 93

The words on the list are a major basis for prepared, stan- · 12 · 34 · 97
dard copy. If you do not use this kind of copy when you practice · 25 · 38 · 101
keying, the use of one copy compared with another can provide · 37 · 42 · 105
conflicting results. Copy that you key for practice is often · 50 · 46 · 110
prepared from the list of common words you just practiced. Copy · 63 · 51 · 114
is rated from easy to difficult. Writings at the average level · 75 · 55 · 118
are often used in writings that are timed. For example, all of · 88 · 59 · 122
the writings in this part of the book are on the average level. · 101 · 63 · 127

gwam 1' 3' | 1 | 2 | 3 | 4 | 5 | 6 | 7 | 8 | 9 | 10 | 11 | 12 | 13 |

Timed Writings
*(3'- and 5'-timed
writings continued)*

32. YOUR COMFORT LEVEL

gwam 3'

The comfort level for keyboarding lies between the levels	4	50
of speed and control. For example, if you work at a rate that	8	55
is between your fastest speed and one that gives the most con-	12	59
trol, you are at your comfort level. This is the rate with	16	63
which you should key your regular work, not the rate you use when	21	67
keying a timed writing or drill to build your speed and control.	25	71
Thus, it is the level at which you have a feeling of ease--you	29	76
are not forced to key too fast for speed or too slow for control.	34	80
When you work at this level, you do not feel stress that might	38	84
relate to speed or control. The result is steady, even keying.	42	89
If a good product is your goal, try to key at the comfort level.	46	93

gwam 3' | 1 | 2 | 3 | 4 |

33. KEYING AND THE MOUSE

gwam 3' | 5'

When you key at the computer, you will work with the mouse,	4	2	48
an input device. Its shape is not always the same. It has more	8	5	51
than one button, but you will mainly use the left button. If you	13	8	53
use your left hand, it can be changed so that you may use the	17	10	56
right button. After working with the mouse, you know that the	21	13	58
main process is to point at a place on the monitor and then click	26	15	61
one or two times to get the results that are needed. The rate	30	18	64
with which the mouse will point and click can be adjusted. Some	34	20	66
of the file items you can point to include open, save, and close.	38	23	69
Now that you know something about the mouse and its use, how	42	25	71
do you work with it? At first you may feel that you cannot con-	47	28	74
trol the mouse. With practice it is as easy as pointing your	51	30	76
finger. You also need to learn to keep the mouse in the center	55	33	79
of your mouse pad and to point and click quickly. You must be	59	36	81
able to point quickly to a place that you select on the monitor.	64	38	84
Once you point to the place that is correct, you are ready to use	68	41	87
the button. You then need to click one or two times. In either	72	43	89
case, press and let go of the button at a very fast rate.	76	46	91

*Timed writings contin-
ued on next page.*

gwam 3'
5'

Drill 12
(continued)

Tenth 100 Words

age mutual classes radio efforts touch previous toward television away legal add color hotel sheets portion ordered revenue capital located daily simply ahead longer purchased transportation weekly

boys payable covered source printed west kindness arrange brought civil engineering goods told referred points mortgage lease banks actual example speed press assured marketing professional trouble

thing university fund grade bond appear secretary travel valuable manufacturing range forwarded cut code base appropriate otherwise maximum thus quantity responsibility congress faculty side behalf

completely stores follow decision considerable insured west legal higher ability town everything officers adequate accident central branch earliest employee actually economic meetings banks arrange

gwam 1' | 1 | 2 | 3 | 4 | 5 | 6 | 7 | 8 | 9 | 10 | 11 | 12 | 13 |

Eleventh 100 Words

aid main relative stated fast increases directors carefully lower club doubt hard teacher safety published presented nothing larger aware red tire I'm inform refer officer license begin extend term

appears motor road instead shows quickly offering analysis useful blank performance reported salary thanking damage dollar checking wrote develop procedures words indeed contracts budget literature

charged story authority types served release church chapter phone appointment applied educational substantial recommend twenty foot promotion design improvement knowledge fiscal whom survey courses

endorsement requesting chance authorized risk subscription single build replacement sufficient includes entitled almost story wrote exchange applications difficult informed whatever sincere evening

gwam 1' | 1 | 2 | 3 | 4 | 5 | 6 | 7 | 8 | 9 | 10 | 11 | 12 | 13 |

Drill 12 continued on next page.

TIMED

Timed Writings
*(3'- and 5'-timed
writings continued)*

34. BASIC KEYING SKILLS

gwam 3'

Before you start any type of job where you use the keyboard,	4 | 51
you must build your keying skills to a proper level. One of the	8 | 56
most needed skills is the quick use of the enter key with steady	13 | 60
motion before, during, and after its use. A similar process is	17 | 64
needed for other special keys that are used very often. Examples	21 | 69
are the space bar, the tab key, and the shift. You also need to	26 | 73
learn the position of the letters and the proper finger to use	30 | 77
with each one of them. For success you should be able to easily	34 | 81
key short words, phrases, and sentences. Also, you should try to	39 | 86
keep in mind the whole process for proper keying that you have	43 | 90
learned as you do your work every day at school and on the job.	47 | 94

gwam 3' | 1 | 2 | 3 | 4 |

35. KEYING MYTHS IN CLASS

gwam 3' | 5'

To learn how to key the right way, practice is the answer.	4 | 2 | 49
This is a myth unless you learn to do the right kind of practice.	9 | 5 | 51
Practice with purpose and meaning is needed to key the right way.	13 | 8 | 54
A story has been told about a class in which all of the students	17 | 10 | 57
were able to key far above the speed and control level that was	22 | 13 | 59
expected by the end of the first school term. During this time,	26 | 16 | 62
the class only worked with timed writings on the letter keys.	30 | 18 | 64
This is a very sad story. The extent of the content was too	34 | 21 | 67
narrow and the practice did not have real purpose and meaning.	39 | 23 | 69
When you learn to key, watch out for myths that might keep	43 | 26 | 72
you from working in the best way. For instance, when you try to	47 | 28 | 74
develop the skill to key, you do not work on speed and control at	51 | 31 | 77
the very same time. You often need to move from your best speed	56 | 33 | 80
level to a slower speed level at which you can have the best con-	60 | 36 | 82
trol. It will confuse you if you try to attain your best speed	64 | 38 | 85
and control at the same time. While it is often good to compete	68 | 41 | 87
in sports, it is a myth that competing with others improves key-	73 | 44 | 90
ing speed or control. Compete only against yourself when keying.	77 | 46 | 92

*Timed writings contin-
ued on next page.*

gwam 3' | 1 | 2 | 3 | 4 |
      5' | 1 | 2 | 3 |

Drill 12
(continued)

Ninth 100 Words

deal fair seems profit miss invitation housing supplies procedure checks bills provisions active claims organizations separate food developed samples personally level industrial article carbon feet

concerned dozen spring growth maintenance left handle acknowledge campaign court permit facts steel manner indicate agents chairman offered kindly self cards asking instructions manual season share

start retail conference foreign distribution serving filing close third makes private returning comments children test particularly apply accordance extended greater teaching trip friends furnished

volume respect known agree based basic carry series title offered progress correspondence around inch added files seeing commercial purposes shipping determined features factory demand fully claims

gwam 1' | 1 | 2 | 3 | 4 | 5 | 6 | 7 | 8 | 9 | 10 | 11 | 12 | 13 |

First 900 Words

gwam 1' | 3'

	1'	3'
Several features are important to consider in looking for a	12	4	67
school. One of these is to consider if the school will provide	25	8	72
for your particular needs. If the need is planning for a future	38	13	76
job, you should know about the course of study and the teachers	51	17	80
with whom you will work. You may want to increase your general	63	21	85
education along with planning for a job. Make a list of your	76	25	89
needs before you determine which school that you will attend.	88	30	93

Several features are important to consider in looking for a school. One of these is to consider if the school will provide for your particular needs. If the need is planning for a future job, you should know about the course of study and the teachers with whom you will work. You may want to increase your general education along with planning for a job. Make a list of your needs before you determine which school that you will attend.

Once you have a school in mind, the process of successful progress is important. Ask for information from other students who have taken a similar course of study. Do not try to answer each question on your own--ask the teachers and the management of the school for help. Plan to study at regular times and write out a schedule, if necessary. The schedule should include time for your personal needs. How well you plan the schedule and how well you follow it should help determine your success in school.

	1'	3'
Once you have a school in mind, the process of successful	12	33	97
progress is important. Ask for information from other students	24	38	101
who have taken a similar course of study. Do not try to answer	37	42	105
each question on your own--ask the teachers and the management of	50	46	110
the school for help. Plan to study at regular times and write	63	51	114
out a schedule, if necessary. The schedule should include time	76	55	118
for your personal needs. How well you plan the schedule and how	88	59	122
well you follow it should help determine your success in school.	100	63	127

Drill 12 continued on next page.

gwam 1' | 1 | 2 | 3 | 4 | 5 | 6 | 7 | 8 | 9 | 10 | 11 | 12 | 13 |
3' | 1 | 2 | 3 | 4 |

TIMED

Timed Writings
*(3'- and 5'-timed
writings continued)*

36. TRANSPOSITION ERRORS
gwam 3'

A transposition error occurs when letters are not keyed in	4	52
proper position next to each other in a word. This is one of the	8	56
most common types of errors that is made. It may be hard to know	13	60
when this type of error is made as you key. Some words are more	17	65
likely to cause this type of error. For example, a word with two	22	69
letters next to each other that are keyed with the same fingers	26	73
on each hand may cause a problem. These errors are often made in	30	78
short, easy words when the word patterns are not yet set well in	35	82
your technique. Work this out by keying this type of word on the	39	86
letter level. You should think of each letter of the word first;	43	91
then think of the whole word. Use special drills, if they help.	48	95

gwam 3' | 1 | 2 | 3 | 4 |

37. KEYING MYTHS ON THE JOB
gwam 3' | 5'

Did you know a test given to check how fast a person keys	4	2	47
does not always show if that person is able to do well on the	8	5	50
job? It is a myth to assume that how one keys on one or two	12	7	52
writings can reveal much about how one would key on the job as	16	10	55
a whole. It has been found in studies about keying that the	20	12	57
skill to do good work on a writing under time does not correlate	25	15	60
to a great extent to how well various types of documents in a	29	17	62
firm are keyed. Too many other factors, like work habits and ef-	33	20	65
ficiency, will affect the success of a person who keys on a job.	37	22	67
At times, you may key copy in which your fingers seem to	41	25	70
move with much ease. At other times, your fingers may not seem	45	27	72
to want to work for you. Do you think that you are not having a	50	30	75
good day when your fingers do not move as you wish? That notion	54	32	78
is one more myth. How hard the copy is can cause problems. Copy	59	35	80
often ranges from an easy level to a much harder level. The dif-	63	38	83
ficulty level of the copy can be often gauged by the types of	67	40	85
words in the copy. Thus, you are most likely not having a good	71	43	88
or bad day; it may be the level of the copy you are keying.	75	45	90

*Timed writings contin-
ued on next page.*

*gwam 3'
5'* | 1 | 2 | 3 | 4 |

SKILLBUILDING

Drill 12 •
High-Frequency Words

1. Refer to Part 1—Basic Level Keyboarding, page 12, for information about high-frequency word drills.

2. To increase your speed, key each of the eight groups of drills on this page and then continue through page 78.

3. Repeat all of Drill 12 if time permits.

Seventh 100 Words

fee try mind taking house estate called financial teachers prompt data net quite signed giving summer terms effect correct car ship assure regulations north things united follows discount excellent

results review big person plus major extra standard freight units understanding least buy lot sign delay catalog events opinion run showing method space hearing land agent man proper schools unless

promptly suggestions research fall health persons successful firm consider according operating throughout expense country something prepared mailing approved outstanding included electric addressed

accept remain corporation handling advance coverage success using certificate examination interesting advised yourself called lines anything herewith programs although hesitate excellent throughout

gwam 1' | 1 | 2 | 3 | 4 | 5 | 6 | 7 | 8 | 9 | 10 | 11 | 12 | 13 |

Eighth 100 Words

easy parts assist clear million process regret specific suggested truck sorry later near bulletin activities continued bureau ready obtain early it's south welcome greatly express discussed medical

among deposit fire gas require postage news obligation conditions machines mailed force hold enclose gives details charges involved condition booklet established placed methods appreciation picture

regard taxes security top farm hours mentioned offices accounting brochure advantage friend idea head morning limited coming center directly provides remember view dollars especially getting except

similar practice satisfactory minimum final late arrangements war different payments submitted accounts council considered proposal station ideas designed expenses selling beginning save obligation

gwam 1' | 1 | 2 | 3 | 4 | 5 | 6 | 7 | 8 | 9 | 10 | 11 | 12 | 13 |

Drill 12 continued on next page.

Timed Writings
*(3'- and 5'-timed
writings continued)*

38. SPECIAL DRILLS

gwam 3'

Drill practice is a good way to help you with speed and con-	4	51
trol. To get the most out of your work, use the drills that may	8	55
help you with the most common types of problems. Finger and row	13	60
drills are very often used. You may need to work with the first,	17	64
second, third, and fourth fingers. You may also practice with	21	68
the first, second, third, and fourth rows. Work on the use of	25	72
the shift for capital letters is also needed. Work with double	30	77
letters and side-by-side letters, as these letters often cause	34	81
problems in words. When you key, spacing may be a major concern.	38	85
As you try to space in the right way, more drill practice in use	43	90
of the space bar may help. Work on what seems to help the most.	47	94

gwam 3' | 1 | 2 | 3 | 4 |

39. KEYING IN THE FUTURE

gwam 3' | 5'

Most experts think that how we key in the future will	4	2	47
change little, if at all, from how we key now. Most anyone who	8	5	50
makes a study of the future will agree there will be new products	12	7	52
and changes in present ones that relate to keying. Even as these	17	10	55
changes take place, it seems that keying will not show a great	21	13	58
deal of change. Even with changes in different types of products	25	15	60
over the years, the place of the keys on a keyboard has had very	30	18	63
little change. This is the case even after studies show a heavy	34	20	65
load is on the left hand and the weaker fingers when one keys.	38	23	68
Have you thought about what is new now and how it will af-	42	25	70
fect those who key on the job or at home? More use of the Inter-	46	28	73
net will greatly affect how we do our work and have fun. When	50	30	75
you simply key an item in a search, the writings of experts can	55	33	78
be brought to you at work or home. Also, e-mail makes it as easy	59	35	81
to key a note to a friend far away as it is to a friend in a	63	38	83
local area. Even with voice input, keying will still be needed	67	40	86
to help edit copy. More use will be made of software that checks	72	43	88
your skill to key and helps you improve that skill.	75	45	90

*Timed writings contin-
ued on next page.*

gwam 3' | 1 | 2 | 3 | 4 |
        5' | 1 | 2 | 3 |

Drill 11
(continued)

*Review G—Shift Key/
Caps Lock*
Read the Technique Tip on
page 69.

Key the drill once for speed.
Rekey the drill for accuracy.

Left Shift

Jo worked at U-Love my Movies; Liz worked at Ole Ocean Park, Inc.
Jammie and Patsy flew to Hawaii and then to Maui, Hilo, and Oahu.
John and May met Ken and Kay at the Jazz Musical Parade in Miami.

Right Shift

Ray, Eve, Sam, and Beth perform in December at Wests Arts Center.
Brown and Smart Software moved in December to Fifth South Avenue.
The World Computer Trade Show starts in Atlantic City on April 5.

Both Shifts

Joe and Randi drove to Orlando to meet James and Eve on March 15.
Paula Weston visited factories in Japan, South Korea, and Taiwan.
The Kea Choir sang at Johnson City Hall in San Jose during April.

Caps Lock

CAPS LOCK is needed to key: ABC, CBS, NBC, CNBC, CNN, and ESPN2.
Selected PC stocks are AAPL, BTWS, DELL, GTW, PVAT, IBM, and CPQ.
ZIP CODE 72704 is for ELKS OK; 45678 OAKS WA; and 88793 BOWIE TX.

gwam 1' | 1 | 2 | 3 | 4 | 5 | 6 | 7 | 8 | 9 | 10 | 11 | 12 | 13 |

Review H—Spacing
Read the Technique Tip on
page 70.

Key the drill once for speed.
Rekey the drill for accuracy.

Spacing

Take my new book, as I was not able to meet you at your set time.
Go to the car and find the tag for it is now good for use by you.
The time is near for me to take a turn in doing the task for you.

Bill needed all of the help that could be given for the meetings.
It is time for Alana to secure a change in venue for a new trial.
Susan reported the musical score and the choir were highly rated.

I won! Who is losing? Therefore, set their seminar at 5:00 p.m.
The Courier font (12pt) was used. Sales grew 12% over last year.
Ray Wise, M.D., and Marion Park, R.N., attended the MDRN meeting.

gwam 1' | 1 | 2 | 3 | 4 | 5 | 6 | 7 | 8 | 9 | 10 | 11 | 12 | 13 |

TIMED

  A

40. ORAL COMMUNICATIONS

gwam 3'

To orally communicate in an effective way is an asset to	4	50
you. To simply get a point across, you frequently need to talk	8	55
with others in a clear and concise manner. You may play a vital	12	59
role as telephone and video conference calls become more and	17	63
more common. Voice mail and answering machines will be used by	21	67
nearly everyone. In situations like these where your voice is	25	71
recorded, you must convey what you think in a kind and courteous	29	76
manner. If you ever use voice-activated input with the personal	34	80
computer, you will speak words rather than key them. Thus, you	38	84
should try to use good grammar at all times. You must also think	42	89
quickly so that you will always speak with meaningful content.	46	93

gwam 3' | 1 | 2 | 3 | 4 |

41. WORKING RELATIONS

gwam 3' | 5'

Good working relations do not happen by accident. To ensure	4	2	48
good working relations, it takes a great deal of effort. Can you	9	5	51
envision people with whom you need to relate well at your job?	13	8	53
As people often interact on the job, they must very firmly grasp	17	10	56
how to interact with others in varied groups. One group is com-	21	13	58
prised of employees. Another group is comprised of employers.	26	15	61
Also, people to whom a firm markets its goods and services is	30	18	63
another group with whom working relations occur. In all cases,	34	20	66
it is wise to possess good working relations with other people.	38	23	68
Once you comprehend what working relations are desirable in	42	25	71
firms, how do you maintain steady, positive working relations	46	28	73
with other people? First, you need to know yourself well enough	51	30	76
to overcome any negative feelings so that only positive feelings	55	33	78
affect your attitude on the job. Second, you need to perceive	59	36	81
that most other people are often trying to pursue a similar path	64	38	84
in having good relations on the job. Third, do not allow one	68	41	86
bad incident to keep you from taking an overall positive view to	72	43	89
seek good working relations with other people on the job.	76	45	91

*Timed writings contin-
ued on next page.*

gwam 3'
5'

Drill 11
(continued)

Review E—Specific Fingers/Rows
Read the Technique Tips on pages 66 and 67.

To improve accuracy, key each group of Review E drills. Rekey words or lines that cause you difficulty.

First/Second Fingers

might return/future flight/may fly/kicked into/did drink/ice dock
The number of guests might change from forty to fifty by tonight.
Eddie decided to keep on doing kind deeds for the needy children.

Third/Fourth Fingers

so low/always look/were old/happy puppy/puzzle parts/azure papers
We will exercise and plan proper snacks that will help our looks.
We quiz many sales applicants who apply in all appropriate areas.

Bottom/Second Rows

can box/minimum ban/zone number/half faded/sells flash/had laughs
My box of nine bananas and five zucchinis can be moved to my van.
Sal asked for a half glass of soda; Dallas had a fast food salad.

Third/Fourth Rows

poor review/your own/party support/score of 15 to 29/#40179862353
Write your poetry without errors as you key it for fourth period.
Send $2,457.69 in 30 days (April 18).   Store sixteen (16) mowers.

gwam 1' | 1 | 2 | 3 | 4 | 5 | 6 | 7 | 8 | 9 | 10 | 11 | 12 | 13 |

Review F—Opposite Hand
Read the Technique Tip on page 68.

To improve accuracy, key each group of Review F drills. Rekey any words, phrases, or sentences that cause you difficulty.

dk/kd and ei/ie

damask raked dusk knowledge desk/ceiling fried deceive identified
baked pie/eight ducks/markdown receipt/faked policies/diet worked
Acknowledge that a chief concern when keyboarding is quiet hands.

sl/ls and ru/ur

slot perils slush hillside aisle/true ruins truck surge truce run
rural hillside/slow turn/also cured/rushing falls/lesson resource
The structures on the rugged hillsides on the island were burned.

ty/yt and wo/ow

quantity anything duty daytime type/woe low world flows row awoke
duty toward/worried youth/typical workweek/would empty/own styles
I know about typical growth of the wool industry in Byten County.

gwam 1' | 1 | 2 | 3 | 4 | 5 | 6 | 7 | 8 | 9 | 10 | 11 | 12 | 13 |

Drill 11 continued on next page.

Timed Writings
(3'- and 5'-timed writings continued)

  A

42. POSITIVE THINKING
gwam 3'

Positive thinking is very important as it has a great effect	4 51
on the attitude of oneself and others. For instance, a person	8 55
who thinks in a positive way often helps others to think in the	13 59
same way. However, negative thinking often causes a person to be	17 64
bitter and not a good influence on others. Positive thinking is	21 68
the way of thinking that is favored by people who study the pro-	26 72
cess of thinking. For instance, experts in the field of psycho-	30 77
logy think that persons need to make a special effort to practice	34 81
positive thinking. Studies by these experts often reflect that	38 85
most persons are both positive and negative in how they react to	43 90
specific issues, but positive thinking is more often dominate.	47 94

gwam 3' | 1 | 2 | 3 | 4 |

43. KINDNESS AT WORK
gwam 3' 5'

Have you ever worked in a firm where you and perhaps others	4 2 48
were dealt with in an unkind manner? You probably can be assured	8 5 50
that this firm had internal dilemmas that were expressed exter-	13 8 53
nally. There were likely some employees in the firm who were un-	17 10 55
able to detach their personal lives from their business lives.	21 13 58
They may have been inclined to inflict their frustrations on	25 15 60
others. Such people may be unkind to the point of being unpro-	29 18 63
fessional. A person who has been treated so unkindly on the job	34 20 65
may finally decide to leave the firm and not come back.	37 22 68
There are not any excuses for lack of kindness within firms,	41 25 70
but it is a reality. Different types of unkind actions can occur	46 27 73
among various personnel. If you are the one at whom these acts	50 30 75
are aimed, think first about what may have caused such actions.	54 33 78
Regardless of whether you are the cause, a calm talk with the	59 35 80
other personnel involved is often helpful. When it is not pos-	63 38 83
sible to resolve the problem, you may wish to discuss the issue	67 40 85
with your supervisor. Guidance from your supervisor about the	71 43 88
problem could prove very helpful to you and the others involved.	75 45 90

Timed writings continued on next page.

gwam 3' 5' | 1 | 2 | 3 | 4 |

SKILLBUILDING

Drill 11
(continued)

Review C—Direct Reach
Read the Technique Tip on page 64.

To improve accuracy, key each group of Review C drills. Rekey words that cause you difficulty.

s-w/j-u/g-t/h-n/d-e/f-v

swamp swift sway sword swept swap/juice jungle juror junior judge
get height gut night gate sight/hand technical hang handle hankie
defy deaf debit decal cadet ideas/favor five fever favorite fives

j-m/a-z/l-./k-,/f-r/s-x/a-q

jamb jump jumbo pajama jumble jam/razed hazy lazy dazed gaze maze
oil. rail. foil./back, pick, ask,/frog fruit fragile afraid frail
six saxophone sox sextet sixth sax/aqua aquaplanes opaque plaques

g-b/k-i/h-y/d-c/l-o/p-;

gab tugboat gable songbird gabby/king ski skip kitchen skit skies
shy hydro hydrant why hymn hybrid/decks medicate wildcats redcoat
lose lock lobe close along locale/drop; equip; lamp; shop; scrap;

Combination

swat swim/jump just/eight get/hand hang/defy cadet/favor favorite
jam jump/jazz haze/sail. oil./ask, sick,/fry from/six sextet/aqua
opaque/gab gable/kinds skit/shy why/dice deck/load lob/top; trap;

gwam 1' | 1 | 2 | 3 | 4 | 5 | 6 | 7 | 8 | 9 | 10 | 11 | 12 | 13 |

Review D—Double Letter
Read the Technique Tip on page 65.

To improve accuracy, key each group of Review D drills. Rekey words that cause you difficulty.

cc/rr and dd/ee

success account occupy accompany/narrow arrows berry horror carry
middle paddles sudden fiddlers/peer deed three deep seem fee meet
Suddenly a squirrel was in a tree and raccoons were by the creek.

ff/pp and ll/nn

waffle different cuff tariff off/upper reapply copper apple happy
tell college ballot will call ill/inner sunny tanner cannot funny
I am planning on annual support of a different college next fall.

mm/ss and tt/oo

hammer tummy mammal comment mummer/assign guess brass mess lesson
cattle witty putts tittle rattle/noon food groom looks cook books
Is it too soon for a comment to the press on the rookie attorney?

Drill 11 continued on next page.

gwam 1' | 1 | 2 | 3 | 4 | 5 | 6 | 7 | 8 | 9 | 10 | 11 | 12 | 13 |

Timed Writings
(3'- and 5'-timed writings continued)

  A

44. PERSONAL HYGIENE

gwam 3'

Maintaining good personal hygiene is essential for pre-	4 | 50
serving your health and your professional reputation. Not only	8 | 54
is poor personal hygiene bad for a person, but others with whom	12 | 58
the person works are also in direct contact with the problems of	17 | 63
poor health habits. Clean and neat clothes are very important to	21 | 67
a person on and off the job. However, good personal hygiene is	25 | 71
more than the appearance of a person. It includes the cleanli-	29 | 75
ness of the body, the hair, the teeth, and other areas. A great	34 | 80
deal of tact is needed to help someone improve personal hygiene.	38 | 84
At times the person who practices habits of poor personal hygiene	42 | 89
is the very last person to realize that a problem exists.	46 | 92

gwam 3' | 1 | 2 | 3 | 4 |

45. PROFESSIONAL DRESS

gwam 3' \| 5'

Although many firms do not have a written dress code, there	4 | 2 | 48
is an unwritten code. You will simply feel out of place on the	8 | 5 | 50
job if you wear clothes that are not appropriate. The type of	13 | 8 | 53
professional dress expected can often be determined by what the	17 | 10 | 55
people on the job are wearing. Mainly, the decision becomes one	21 | 13 | 58
of good taste. In other words, wear what seems to be most pro-	25 | 15 | 60
fessional and acceptable at your firm. In some firms, the dress	30 | 18 | 63
has already been dictated by use of certain types of uniforms.	34 | 20 | 65
Acceptable professional dress is important for your success.	38 | 23 | 68
Once an employee understands what is acceptable dress on	42 | 25 | 70
the job, meeting the requirements of dress is not always easy.	46 | 28 | 73
In certain cases, a new job may mean added expenses to purchase	50 | 30 | 75
clothes to augment your present ones. In making these purchases	55 | 33 | 78
or using clothing already owned, you must be careful not to over-	59 | 35 | 80
dress or underdress. You should not attempt to stand out from	63 | 38 | 83
others in your professional wear, unless your job calls for you	67 | 40 | 86
to. Try to keep your working wardrobe acceptable by always keep-	72 | 43 | 88
ing it cleaned and pressed and by adding to it slowly.	75 | 45 | 90

Timed writings continued on next page.

gwam 3' | 1 | 2 | 3 | 4 |
5' | 1 | 2 | 3 |

Drill 11 •
Drill Practice Review

Review A—Adjacent Keys
Read the Technique Tip on
page 62.

Concentrate on the empha-
sized pair.

FEATURE: Emphasizes the following categories: Adjacent Keys, Concentration, Direct
Reach, Double Letter, Specific Fingers/Rows, Opposite Hand, Shift Key/Caps Lock, and
Spacing.

BENEFIT: Reinforce stroking techniques in eight categories of common keying errors.

TECHNIQUE TIP: Keep fingers curved and upright.

GOAL: To maintain control when keying each of the drills.

as/sa and er/re

asa areas sale least say tasks **ere** after great under reply serves
repay cash/every lease/salty water/merely asked/real as/were read
Please repay cash for water services after the great sauna sales.

rt/tr and io/oi

rtr part treaty forth straw short **ioi** prior coin motion oil lions
extra support/prior choice/radio report/start doing/trade cartons
Our choice is to stress extra court support for violent behavior.

ew/we and op/po

ewe sew went knew owe grew lower **opo** copy import opted spot crops
grew crops/weak power/opposite view/weird poll/new hope/drew upon
As we knew about the wet weather, we stopped for the new ponchos.

gwam 1' | 1 | 2 | 3 | 4 | 5 | 6 | 7 | 8 | 9 | 10 | 11 | 12 | 13 |

Review B—Concentration
Read the Technique Tip on
page 63.

To improve accuracy, key each
group of Review B drills. If
you make an error in a line,
rekey the line one or more
times.

Complex Words, Transposition, and Punctuation Marks

dazed passengers/streetcar swerved/hazards occurred/waxed statues
We waded water as Wes Wedgies drew daringly west of Weaversville.
Estates with acreage averaged a minimum of a million after taxes.

sufficient test/their heirloom/few new/within easy/received taxes
Their neighbor averaged eight visits for which they are incensed.
Effie and Malease deserve their sufficient treks of genuine ease.

Rice and Hay, Inc./P.O. Box 190/B. Clay, M.D./pledge of $1,150.82
Tobie's "gain" shown (line 14) is correct; his "loss" is incorrect.
Scores are: Bo, 11; Jo, 9; and Vi, 16.   Is it true?   It is true!

*Drill 11 continued on
next page.*

gwam 1' | 1 | 2 | 3 | 4 | 5 | 6 | 7 | 8 | 9 | 10 | 11 | 12 | 13 |

TIMED

Timed Writings
(3'- and 5'-timed writings continued)

46. PERSONALITY TRAITS

gwam 3'

Personality is the totality of the non-physical traits of a	4	50
person. Thus, personality is often reflected in the total of	8	54
good and bad traits of a person. In some people, these traits	12	58
tend to surface very quickly. In others, the traits are more	17	63
subtle and surface more slowly. Some tests can measure a per-	21	67
son's relative good and bad traits. However, how honest a person	25	71
is in answering questions on the tests will often have an effect	29	75
on how valid and reliable these tests are. Over a reasonable	33	79
period of time, the personality of a person can often be observed	38	84
with more meaning. However, how a person acts does not always	42	88
reveal much about how he or she really feels in a situation.	46	92

gwam 3' | 1 | 2 | 3 | 4 |

47. BUSINESS MANNERS

gwam 3' | 5'

In a business, a supervisor's manners toward an employee	4	2	47
depend on very simple rules of good etiquette. A friendly and	8	5	50
gracious attitude is a form of good etiquette. Such an attitude	12	7	53
can form the basis of a good working relationship. The kinds of	17	10	55
actions that a supervisor exhibits will likely be returned. As	21	13	58
the supervisor, it is up to you to demonstrate the kind of busi-	25	15	60
ness manners you wish employees to copy. This may not be easy,	29	18	63
but it often is a very rewarding experience. In the short and	34	20	65
the long run, good business manners will pay off for you.	37	22	68
Similarly, an employee's manners toward a supervisor also	41	25	70
depend on some simple rules of good etiquette. Listening very	46	27	72
closely to what is expected of you is a form of good manners. In	50	30	75
most instances, a supervisor expects you to work through proper	54	33	78
channels when dealing with persons on higher levels. This means	59	35	80
that your own supervisor is most often the first channel for	63	38	83
clearing your work, unless you have other instructions. A super-	67	40	85
visor expects you to always be on time and work hard. You are	71	43	88
then on your way to becoming a respected, well-liked employee.	75	45	90

Timed writings continued on next page.

gwam 3' | 1 | 2 | 3 | 4 |
5' | 1 | 2 | 3 |

Drill 10 •
Spacing

Key each drill once for speed; rekey each drill for accuracy.

FEATURE: Emphasizes use of the space bar with short words and phrases, sentences, and punctuation and symbols.

BENEFIT: Improve stroking technique.

TECHNIQUE TIP: Tap the space bar with a quick down-and-in motion with the right thumb.

GOAL: To space correctly between words.

Short Words and Phrases

be do of for no the to put am can go was at we ad as our an by on
if it/we can/by the/a pet/go to/do you/let me/no way/own it/be on
but we can/by the box/fed my dog/you and me/he hit it/get our oil

and home way boat bat race sow base cat want pad saw drag fit sit
many can/one acre/dog food/pet cats/long naps/lake area/much more
some may race/our best aide/web site/she came home/sew your shirt

gwam 1' | 1 | 2 | 3 | 4 | 5 | 6 | 7 | 8 | 9 | 10 | 11 | 12 | 13 |

Sentences

As you own a new car, we may buy a road map to put in it for you.
A mode to save is to use a part of what you earn to help it grow.
If you want to do a job in the right way, set good goals to meet.

Joan wanted to know what caused the problem with the tank of gas.
The movie was just the right length for Vi to have a spicy pizza.
As a result of snow, Ed wanted to set a new time for the meeting.

gwam 1' | 1 | 2 | 3 | 4 | 5 | 6 | 7 | 8 | 9 | 10 | 11 | 12 | 13 |

Punctuation and Symbols

The end-of-year net loss is $48; last year's net loss was $2,177.
Mrs. Bern said: "Bern & Cole, Inc. grew 10% in sales this year."
Who lost? I'm excited! Remember, a flight (923) is at 4:00 p.m.

Help! Do we know? Roy sees. Tom could. Win will. Val's here.
That's impossible! John--a likeable person--is an M.D. in Texas.
The cost is $189.50 per load today; it was $168.81 late Saturday.

gwam 1' | 1 | 2 | 3 | 4 | 5 | 6 | 7 | 8 | 9 | 10 | 11 | 12 | 13 |

Timed Writings
(3'- and 5'-timed writings continued)

48. TEAMWORK AND GOALS

gwam 3'

Sports events are often won as a result of teamwork. They | 4 | 51
are often lost when there is a lack of teamwork. Working as a | 8 | 55
team is very important in many situations. As a result of good | 12 | 59
planning, most organizations have long- and short-term goals. In | 17 | 64
most cases, each of the goals is easier to attain with a team ef- | 21 | 68
fort. When hiring new employees, most organizations try to re- | 25 | 72
cruit persons who will work as members of a team in sharing the | 30 | 76
common goals that have been established. Persons are out of step | 34 | 81
when their goals are inconsistent with those of the organization. | 38 | 85
Although you need to develop your own goals, the goals of the | 43 | 89
organization in which you are employed are also very significant. | 47 | 94

gwam 3' | 1 | 2 | 3 | 4 |

49. MOTIVATION AT WORK

gwam 3' | 5'

When a person is encouraged, that person is often strongly | 4 | 2 | 48
motivated. One of the best kinds of encouragement is that which | 8 | 5 | 50
ensues from intrinsic or internal motivation. When a person does | 13 | 8 | 53
a good job, this often results in good feelings. For instance, | 17 | 10 | 56
to complete a job that was not easy is often a form of encourage- | 21 | 13 | 58
ment that is internal. A person is often encouraged by finishing | 26 | 15 | 61
a routine job within less time than is expected. Thus, if a per- | 30 | 18 | 63
son performs beyond what is expected in a job, the person may be | 34 | 21 | 66
encouraged to proceed in doing an even better job next time. | 38 | 23 | 68

Another method that is used to encourage a person is ex- | 42 | 25 | 71
trinsic or external motivation. For instance, once a good job is | 46 | 28 | 73
done, the person finishing the job is provided with one or more | 51 | 30 | 76
tangible items for recognition. This type of motivation, which | 55 | 33 | 78
is used often on the job, can take several forms. Raises and | 59 | 35 | 81
awards are two examples. Mostly, these are given for job re- | 63 | 38 | 83
lated purposes. Most experts often think that encouragement of | 67 | 40 | 86
this kind is not as strong as that which is internal. Both kinds | 72 | 43 | 88
of encouragement are likely to motivate a person on the job. | 76 | 45 | 91

Timed writings continued on next page.

gwam 3' | 1 | 2 | 3 | 4 |
5' | 1 | 2 | 3 |

Drill 9 •
Shift Key/Caps Lock

Part A
Key each line using a quick
"one-two" rhythm.

FEATURE: Emphasizes left and right shift keys and caps lock.

BENEFIT: Improve technique when shifting and using the caps lock.

TECHNIQUE TIP: Hold down the shift key, key the letter, and release the shift key quickly without pausing. Use quick action in striking and releasing caps lock.

GOAL: To maintain efficiency when using service keys.

Left Shift Key

Kala, Pam, Lana, and Olan will sing at Jons Park in June or July.
In New York she traveled to Ithaca, Kingston, Potsdam, and Utica.
John told Nancy and Jim that he left for Paris on Monday, July 4.

Right Shift Key

The Apple Growers Festival in Damson is on Saturday, September 6.
This year Wes was in Texas, Arizona, Maine, Alabama, and Florida.
Rob and Stan flew to meet Sam and Ron at the WW Roundup Stampede.

Both Shifts

Mark Sole, Keith Ash, and Justin Ziger sold for Weight Line, Inc.
Hanson enrolled in Spanish at Forest Heights Technical Institute.
Ralph, Jud, Dean, and Kit will meet Ray and Louie in Mexico City.

Caps Lock

The TV shows ON and OFF; the VCR shows START, STOP, REC, and REW.
Certain NASDAQ stocks are ORCL, MSFT, NOVL, SUNW, CSCO, and INTC.
NASA and FAA relate to air; USDA, ICC, IRS, and GAO are domestic.

gwam 1' | 1 | 2 | 3 | 4 | 5 | 6 | 7 | 8 | 9 | 10 | 11 | 12 | 13 |

Part B
Key the two paragraphs twice
for control.

Combination   gwam 1'

    The Internet can be traced to ARPANET (Advanced Research   11
Projects Agency Network). Later, a group of scientists at CERN   24
(European Laboratory for Particle Physics) and MIT (Massachusetts   37
Institute of Technology) developed the WWW (World Wide Web).   49

    The Internet is accessed through URLs, short for Uniform   61
Research Locator. At the start of URLs you see the letters http.   74
HTTP (HyperText Transfer Protocol) lets your browser with a GUI   87
(Graphical User Interface) locate a specific WWW Home Page.   99

gwam 1' | 1 | 2 | 3 | 4 | 5 | 6 | 7 | 8 | 9 | 10 | 11 | 12 | 13 |

TIMED

Timed Writings
(3'- and 5'-timed writings continued)

  A

50. EMPLOYEE RELATIONS

gwam 3'

Think of the great amount of time an individual spends on	4	51
the job during a lifetime. You will spend this time either as an	8	55
employee or an employer. Presently, you may or may not be in ei-	13	59
ther one of these roles. Whether you operate your own business	17	64
or work for someone else now or in the future, you will find that	21	68
the relations between an employee and an employer consume a great	26	73
amount of time. Regardless of whether you are an employee or an	30	77
employer, positive relations are needed. To make sure relations	34	81
are positive, an employer must always maintain fair treatment for	39	86
an employee. Similarly, an employee must realize early what is	43	90
required and follow through with the best relations possible.	47	94

gwam 3' | 1 | 2 | 3 | 4 |

51. SELECTING A CAREER

gwam 3' | 5'

How do you select a career that is right for you? You first	4	2	48
need to consider your aptitude and interest for certain careers.	8	5	51
You also need to study different careers. As you study, you will	13	8	53
find various types of sources useful to you. For example, ask	17	10	56
persons why they chose their careers. Try to learn if they are	21	13	58
satisfied or perhaps not satisfied with their choices. Learn	25	15	61
about careers from magazines, books, and pamphlets. Internet	30	18	63
sites with information about careers are helpful. The time you	34	20	66
spend in learning about careers is time that is well spent.	38	23	68
Once you reach a tentative career choice, reconsider what	42	25	71
aptitude and interest you may have in the selected career. When	46	28	73
you consider aptitude, try to discover if you have the ability to	50	30	76
learn and understand the skills and knowledge required in the se-	55	33	78
lected career. If you do not have a real interest in a career,	59	35	81
you most likely will be unhappy in it. Be careful not to select	63	38	84
a career that is short lived or gives very little opportunity for	68	41	86
changing to another career. Even with a good choice, a person is	72	43	89
still likely to change careers several times during a lifetime.	76	46	91

Timed writings continued on next page.

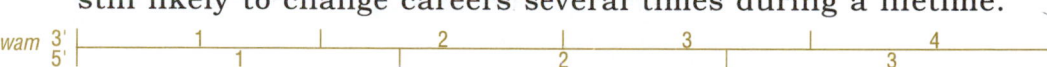
gwam 3' | 1 | 2 | 3 | 4 |
5' | 1 | 2 | 3 |

Drill 8 •
Opposite Hand

To improve accuracy, key each group of drills. If a word, phrase, or sentence causes you difficulty, rekey it immediately one or more times.

FEATURE: Includes common opposite-hand combinations.

BENEFIT: Improve accuracy.

TECHNIQUE TIP: Concentrate on each pair of opposite-hand letters.

GOAL: To maintain control in keying common opposite-hand letters.

dk/kd

dark liked dike asked docket leaked donkey kind duck kidney desks
deck rocked/keyboarding disk/backyard padlock/baked duck/kind kid
At daybreak our parked car skidded backwards as the dike cracked!

ei/ie

their died receipts diesel eighth briefly neither science freight
brief diet/science reviews/receive either/their views/eight piers
She believed the movie receipts were not received on either date.

sl/ls

sled else slender false slice oils slide pulse slight opals slant
sleigh bells/seldom false/falls asleep/slum islands/slow sledding
A slate of slick slogans may improve the slow sales of baseballs.

ru/ur

rung hurt structure truce surged untrue bureau brush during truth
rugged curves/our treasures/rusty urns/suburban tours/rug brushes
She surely sunburned by surfing and running for hours in the sun.

ty/yt

typical myth treaty city empty byte style county activity daytime
typical styles/dirty city/twenty bytes/nutty myths/tyrant tycoons
Youth may typify the quality and style of life in a typical city.

wo/ow

work shown wonder rowing awoke blow worried slow worth window won
slow growth/shown worthy/two owners/own sword/bow works/owl awoke
Your fellow workers have shown their worth toward worried owners.

gwam 1' | 1 | 2 | 3 | 4 | 5 | 6 | 7 | 8 | 9 | 10 | 11 | 12 | 13 |

TIMED

52. TIMELINESS AT WORK

gwam 3'

Timeliness does not happen by chance, but rather is a result	4	54
of good planning and organization. Do you plan and organize your	9	59
time so that you appear promptly at meetings? If your answer is	13	63
"no," you should keep an eye on the clock and leave for your	17	67
meetings early. It is true that some foolish persons appear to	21	71
pride themselves on being late to meetings. However, timeliness	26	76
is a significant trait often fostered by employers. If an em-	30	80
ployee is often late for work, earnings of an employer may be	34	84
affected. Other employees are also often affected if an em-	38	88
ployee is late. They may become upset because they have to do	42	92
another's work. Again, if you have a tendency not to be on time,	46	97
you should seize the opportunity to try to solve the problem.	50	101

gwam 3' | 1 | 2 | 3 | 4 |

53. PATIENCE IS A VIRTUE

gwam 3' | 5'

A person who is capable of calmly awaiting a result or an	4	2	47
outcome is patient. There appears to be a large variation in	8	5	50
patience among employees. Your degree of patience may or may	12	7	52
not be an asset to you on the job. Some employers, frequently	16	10	55
in the field of selling, want people who show some impatience.	21	12	57
The rationale is that persons who are considered too patient will	25	15	60
not work as diligently toward meeting goals that may be set.	29	18	62
Thus, the extent of patience needed to meet job demands varies,	33	20	65
depending on the type of job and the type of people on the job.	38	22	68
Most employers discourage the outward expression of im-	41	25	70
patience. If you know that you are not being patient on a par-	45	27	72
ticular day, try to control it in the same way that you control	50	30	75
other factors that cause problems on your job. Try to conduct	54	32	77
your work in a way that impatience does not have a direct effect	58	35	80
on the job. Achieve balance by understanding that your impa-	62	37	82
tience can cause you to do less than a perfect job. To exhibit	67	40	85
control and balance with patience is a characteristic that will	71	42	87
make your work and your workplace more pleasant and productive.	75	45	90

Timed writings contin-
ued on next page.

gwam 3' | 1 | 2 | 3 | 4 |
         5' | 1 | 2 | 3 |

SKILLBUILDING

Drill 7 •
Specific Rows

Part A
To improve accuracy, key each group of drills. If a word, phrase, or sentence causes you difficulty, rekey it immediately one or more times. Repeat the drill.

FEATURE: Emphasizes a specific row.

BENEFIT: Reinforce key locations and stroking techniques.

TECHNIQUE TIP: Maintain home row position. Keep fingers curved and upright.

GOAL: To strengthen accuracy and reaches.

Bottom Row

van numb civic branch zinc manner bomb excavate maximize box band
main branch/mammoth bomb/my concerns/became amazed/convinced many
To excavate near cabins and zinc mines is a main concern for Max.

Second Row

add hash shall slash salads flags alfalfa falls ask gaffs glasses
last fall/glass flask/fresh alfalfa/an ad/doll sale/stashed aside
A dish of fresh salad was added to the meal for staff and guests.

Third Row

tire quit wrote required worry equity rewrite ripe youth property
proper papers/writer reviewed/your trip/right quotes/youth groups
A reporter reviewed the newspaper story with additional pictures.

Fourth Row

The stock quote was 11 7/16 (9:35 a.m.); only 6 1/4 (2:45 p.m.).
Our figures are: $2,050 x 7.5% = $153.75 and $1,500 x 6% = $90.
Telephone Billy at 555-147-6809 about six o'clock in the evening.

gwam 1' | 1 | 2 | 3 | 4 | 5 | 6 | 7 | 8 | 9 | 10 | 11 | 12 | 13 |

Part B
To improve accuracy, key a 1' writing on each paragraph. As time permits, repeat the drill for accuracy.

Bottom/Second and Third/Fourth Row Paragraphs

gwam 1'

Keyboarding classes should assist with skills in different 12
areas. Speed and accuracy are two of these areas. Speed is 24
achieved as faster finger movements are made. Accuracy is 36
achieved as finger movements are managed at a slower paced rate. 49

Software is preferred to figure speed rates on writings. 12
However, let's take an example of a 3' writing and figure it: 24
Keyed 600 strokes divided by 5 (average word length) equals 120 37
words; and 120 words divided by 3 (3' writing) equals 40 gwam. 49

gwam 1' | 1 | 2 | 3 | 4 | 5 | 6 | 7 | 8 | 9 | 10 | 11 | 12 | 13 |

Timed Writings
(3'- and 5'-timed writings continued)

54. FIRST IMPRESSION

gwam 3'

What do you think about the impression that a person makes	4 | 50
when you first meet him or her? Some persons think that the	8 | 54
first impression is the best way to determine what someone is	12 | 58
like. Think of some of your friends. Was this true of them? In	17 | 63
some instances, you were possibly accurate in analyzing someone	21 | 67
by a first impression. However, in most cases, you will find	25 | 71
that it takes more than the first meeting to discern what a per-	29 | 75
son is like. But the first impression may appear to give you	33 | 79
some idea, especially if a person exhibits negative qualities.	38 | 84
For example, you may observe poor speaking ability, improper	42 | 88
dress, and negative personal traits when you first meet a person.	46 | 92

gwam 3' | 1 | 2 | 3 | 4 |

55. BE A GENUINE PERSON

gwam 3' | 5'

Have you ever purchased a product that includes a guarantee	4 | 2 | 45
that it is genuine? Did you discover later that it was not genu-	8 | 5 | 48
ine? You were probably not happy with the product. You most	12 | 7 | 50
likely returned it for a refund. Unfortunately, dealing with	17 | 10 | 53
people who are not genuine is not as easy as dealing with a prod-	21 | 13 | 55
uct that is not genuine. One of the worst traits a person can	25 | 15 | 58
have is that of not being genuine. A person who isn't genuine is	29 | 18 | 61
insincere in both words and actions and may not be trustworthy.	34 | 20 | 63
How does a lack of genuineness hurt a firm? When firms work	38 | 23 | 66
with the outside world, they try hard to satisfy their custom-	42 | 25 | 68
ers. The same principle holds true for the working relations	46 | 28 | 71
among employees in a firm. If an employee is not genuine, this	50 | 30 | 73
may soon be recognized by other employees. Other employees may	55 | 33 | 76
resent an employee who is not sincere, and this will cause dis-	59 | 35 | 78
harmony in the firm. If the situation persists and affects your	63 | 38 | 81
work, you and others may wish to report it to the supervisor to	67 | 40 | 83
preserve quality customer service and the atmosphere of the firm.	72 | 43 | 86

Timed writings continued on next page.

gwam 3' | 1 | 2 | 3 | 4 |
5' | 1 | 2 | 3 |

Drill 6 •
Specific Fingers

Part A
Key each line once; repeat the drill as time permits.

FEATURE: Emphasizes a specific finger.

BENEFIT: Reinforce key locations and stroking techniques.

TECHNIQUE TIP: Key long reaches with minimum hand movement. Think as you key.

GOAL: To strengthen correct reaches.

First Finger

night hurry my number going young height month knight many return
just right/your job/might try/bringing them/notify my/huge mirror
The months of June or July might be their best time for swimming.

Second Finger

deck keyed deeds cider kind ended idea clerk check jackets needle
were induced/clerk decided/tired elder/decayed seed/cedar pattern
We decided to check on the key kinds of jackets to keep in stock.

Third Finger

solo low looks follows lost explore owl wool gold swallows always
low sales/would allow/six less/local poll/old loans/shallow plots
Show Leo and Lois how to always look and shop for wholesome food.

Fourth Finger

aqua apply happy pop puzzles quartz pleasant azure zipped dazzles
area park/appears happy/pay past/dazzled ape/puppy paw/upper part
Zep was puzzled and dazzled at the quizzes about the pizza place.

gwam 1' | 1 | 2 | 3 | 4 | 5 | 6 | 7 | 8 | 9 | 10 | 11 | 12 | 13 |

Part B
To improve accuracy, key a 1' writing on each paragraph. As time permits, repeat the drill for accuracy.

First/Second and Third/Fourth Finger Paragraphs

gwam 1'

Using the left and right shift keys to key capital letters 12
is often a problem. The left or right shift keys must be quickly 25
held down before striking a key to be capitalized. It is just as 38
important to quickly let go of the shift key after it is used. 51

To properly strike the space bar is absolutely essential 11
for successful operation. For example, pressing the space bar 24
instead of striking it sharply causes new spaces. Failing to 36
grasp rules of proper punctuation also causes spacing problems. 49

gwam 1' | 1 | 2 | 3 | 4 | 5 | 6 | 7 | 8 | 9 | 10 | 11 | 12 | 13 |

Timed Writings
(3'- and 5'-timed writings continued)

  A

56. PRIVACY IS PRICELESS

gwam 3'

	3'	
Can you keep a secret? Businesses often need good employees	4	50
to know some types of information that are of a confidential or a	8	55
private nature. It is common for firms to set policies for keep-	13	59
ing company information confidential. The ability to follow	17	63
policy that keeps such information within the firm is a trait	21	67
that is much desired in an employee. Once private information is	25	72
leaked outside the firm, unfounded rumors may occur, which could	30	76
prove very harmful to a firm. It also could result in a firm	34	80
losing a competitive edge. In addition, an employee to whom a	38	84
leak is attributed may end up in serious trouble. At times,	42	88
leaks by an employee may lead to various types of legal actions.	46	93

gwam 3' | 1 | 2 | 3 | 4 |

57. THE FLEXIBLE WORKER

gwam 3' | 5'

	3'	5'	
Someone who is flexible is most likely to be able to respond	4	2	48
quickly to change. It is very important for a person to respond	8	5	51
to the many changes that can occur on the job. Change sometimes	13	8	53
occurs rapidly and at other times it happens more slowly. Today,	17	10	56
advances in technology tend to create rapid change, especially	21	13	58
in the school and in the office. It is very hard for an inflex-	26	15	61
ible person to effectively adapt to these changes. Most experts	30	18	64
agree that people who are flexible in adapting to change are most	34	21	66
likely to do well in school and to earn promotions in their jobs.	39	23	69
For many years, the manual typewriter was the only choice	43	26	71
in most schools and firms. The electric typewriter became the	47	28	74
best choice some time later. It was possible to correct copy	51	31	76
and save work with the better electronic models that came along	55	33	79
in the eighties. Since then, very simple, then more complex,	59	36	81
computers emerged in the office and in schools. Software made it	64	38	84
quite easy to correct and save large and small documents. Stu-	68	41	86
dents and workers alike adapted well to these changes and remain	72	43	89
flexible as more powerful hardware and software come along.	76	46	91

Timed writings continued on next page.

gwam 3' | 1 | 2 | 3 | 4 |
 5' | 1 | 2 | 3 |

Drill 5 •
Double Letter

To improve accuracy, key each group of drills. If a word or sentence causes you difficulty, rekey it one or more times.

FEATURE: Includes words and sentences with double letters.

BENEFIT: Reinforce stroking techniques with double letters.

TECHNIQUE TIP: Maintain even rhythm; key letters quickly.

GOAL: To maintain control in keying double letters.

cc/rr

occupy current accounting arrives succeed arrange accuse marriage
accept carry accompany hurry occur scurry access borrow vaccinate
Orr arrived to access an array of currently accumulated accounts.

dd/ee

ladder deep odds meeting addle knee hidden feel added deer midday
degree riddle green address feed padded weeds rudder need haddock
A deer was suddenly hidden by a tree near a deep creek at midday.

ff/pp

affect apply office suppose efficient skipped coffee upper effort
supply staff appeals afford stopped offers support differ approve
Our office staff sipped coffee and stopped to approve its appeal.

ll/nn

sells annual allows annoy teller personnel hello winners parallel
banner follows antenna billed flannel poll planning recall dinner
Follow all winners to our annex for annual fall planning ballots.

mm/ss

hammer discuss mummer stress comments pressure immediate sessions
summer issue swimming less summary missed gummy assured committee
Comments about the lesson assignments were stressed in a summary.

tt/oo

watts school battle rookie attorney looked knitting tool settlers
troop kitten groom matter books etiquette pool attach soon butter
Matt must choose two books on good etiquette and woolen knitting.

gwam 1' | 1 | 2 | 3 | 4 | 5 | 6 | 7 | 8 | 9 | 10 | 11 | 12 | 13 |

TIMED

Timed Writings
(3'- and 5'-timed writings continued)

      A

	58. HOW YOU EARN TRUST	*gwam* 3'	

Mostly, trust is a trait that is not quickly noted in a person. Trust is an example of a trait that is earned. To trust a person is to place reliance in the character, ability, or honesty of that person. Therefore, it is easier to trust persons who have demonstrated through varied actions that their trust is warranted. When you expect a person to trust you, the trust is also substantiated by your actions. The real test of trust is whether you or others have proven that trust is genuine and long lasting. As an employer, a primary responsibility is to ascertain whether others in a firm are trusted employees. To be successful, an employee must purposely work in earning the trust of an employer.

	4	51
	8	55
	13	60
	17	64
	21	68
	26	73
	30	77
	34	82
	39	86
	43	90
	47	94

gwam 3' | 1 | 2 | 3 | 4 |

59. CONCERN AND LOYALTY   *gwam* 3' | 5'

Another significant attitude affecting the workplace is that of concern. Too often there seems to be an adversarial relationship, rather than one of concern, between an employee and an employer. Concern needs to be shown by both parties. One way an employer can show concern is to provide an employee with a good salary and good fringe benefits. Employees show concern for their employer by performing their jobs in a way that will help an employer meet the goals of a firm. Employees who do more than what is expected can expect to earn greater rewards.

Loyalty is the employee trait that most shows concern for the employer, according to one survey. Loyalty comes into play when working out problems that are unpleasant in a firm. In other words, it is often very difficult to assess the loyalty of an employee until a critical incident arises in a firm. The character of a person is often shown by the loyalty that is demonstrated in this kind of incident. If an incident of this kind occurs in your firm, you must show your concern by doing your best to show loyalty to your employer by supporting its policies.

	3'	5'	
	4	2	47
	8	5	50
	13	8	52
	17	10	55
	21	13	58
	25	15	60
	29	18	63
	34	20	65
	37	22	07
	41	25	70
	45	27	72
	50	30	75
	54	32	77
	58	35	80
	62	37	82
	66	40	85
	71	42	87
	75	45	90

Timed writings continued on next page.

gwam 3' / 5'

Drill 4 •
Direct Reach

To improve accuracy, key each group of drills. If a specific direct reach in a line causes you difficulty, rekey the line two or more times.

FEATURE: Emphasizes reaches from the home row to the first and third rows.

BENEFIT: Reinforce stroking techniques from the home row.

TECHNIQUE TIP: Key reaches from home row fluently without moving the hand.

GOAL: To maintain control without pausing on the home row.

s-w/j-u/g-t

sws swim swing answer swap swarm swat sweater juj just judge junk adjust juvenile jumps injuries gtg ragtime strength length ragtag Judge the swift and lengthy answers by jurors about the injuries.

h-n/d-e/f-v

hnh doughnut technic technique technology ded decide deck depends dear ideas guide deaf debt fvf favor fever disfavor five favorite De decided to defer five favorite ideas about the debate to John.

j-m/a-z/l-./k-,

jmj jumble jam jumbo jump pajama aza azure jazz dazed gaze azalea l.l foil. oil. retail. sail. k,k back, blank, pick, flank, snack, As Jimmy gazed back, azaleas in the gazebo were jammed in a pail.

f-r/s-x/a-q

frf fresh friends fractures front afraid frost sxs six sox sextet saxophone sixth sexist aqa aqua opaque aquarium plaques aqueducts Fred Fry, a friend, earned a plaque by playing a sax in a sextet.

g-b/k-i/h-y

gbg tugboat strongbox longbow songbird kik kick kite kinds skirts kit kings skim kitchen hyh hymn physical hybrid physician physics Kim, why did kinds of longbows used by kings take physical skill?

d-c/l-o/p-;

dcd grandchild broadcast redcoat wildcat lol lot load along below lower locate loan close color p;p trip; lamp; shop; cap; develop; Their grandchild was located at the shop; my grandchild was lost.

gwam 1' | 1 | 2 | 3 | 4 | 5 | 6 | 7 | 8 | 9 | 10 | 11 | 12 | 13 |

TIMED

Timed Writings
(3'- and 5'-timed writings continued)

---

60. PERSONNEL SELECTION

gwam 3'

When budgets of various firms are analyzed, one of the items	4 | 51
that requires the most expense is that of hiring personnel. Hir-	8 | 55
ing of new personnel is not only very costly, but is also time	13 | 59
consuming. The success or failure of a firm is often gauged by	17 | 64
how well its personnel are hired. Thus, a firm usually closely	21 | 68
examines the work experience and education of a job applicant be-	25 | 72
fore that person is hired. Work experience that relates direct-	30 | 76
ly to the job is often very helpful in the selective process. At	34 | 81
times, work experience not directly related to the job can help.	38 | 85
The formal education of a job applicant also influences the pro-	43 | 89
cess. An interview confirms if the applicant is the best choice.	47 | 94

gwam 3' | 1 | 2 | 3 | 4 |

---

61. MANAGING CONFLICTS

gwam 3' | 5'

Have you ever experienced a real conflict with a person? If	4	2 | 48
you have, this timed writing may take on special meaning for you.	9	5 | 50
If not, the day may come when such a conflict might occur. It	13	8 | 53
is often shocking how quickly a conflict can occur in a firm.	17	10 | 55
You need to show fairness in dealing with others to help prevent	21	13 | 58
conflicts. Conflicts between one employee and another employee	26	15 | 61
and at other times between an employee and an employer often	30	18 | 63
lower the level of production for a firm in which such conflicts	34	20 | 66
occur. A solution to a conflict may sometimes appear harsh.	38	23 | 00
To prevent or to control a conflict, you should try to pre-	42	25 | 70
vent or to slow down the conflict before it reaches a stage that	46	28 | 73
is difficult to correct. Obviously, the best solution is to pre-	51	30 | 76
vent the conflict. Thus, you must stay alert to the dynamics	55	33 | 78
that are taking place around you. Once you think a conflict is	59	35 | 81
going to occur, you and other persons may need to intervene imme-	63	38 | 83
diately. However, if a conflict has already occurred, this is	67	40 | 86
often more serious. In this case, you and other persons must	72	43 | 88
carefully evaluate the situation before trying to intervene.	76	45 | 91

Timed writings continued on next page.

gwam 3' | 1 | 2 | 3 | 4 |
        5' | 1 | 2 | 3 |

Drill 3 •
Concentration

To improve accuracy, key fluently without rushing. Repeat the drill as time permits.

FEATURE: Emphasizes long words, commonly transposed letters, and punctuation.

BENEFIT: Improve accuracy.

TECHNIQUE TIP: Concentrate as you key.

GOAL: To maintain control while keying words that often cause errors.

Complex Sentences

Zebras barely teetered on a rugged terrain of stones and pebbles.
Bedazzled Vi jumped from diving boards in brightly lighted pools.
Repeated research reported ruthlessly ravaged, ransacked regalia.

Faxed warrants warned parolees, namely, systematically occurring.
Mentors graciously serve students, e.g., specialized conferences.
Poets were awesomely intense, i.e., overpowering to participants.

gwam 1' | 1 | 2 | 3 | 4 | 5 | 6 | 7 | 8 | 9 | 10 | 11 | 12 | 13 |

Commonly Transposed Letters

tea eat us using to of the then ten next as said few new be being
were we in it are ware at on or for tow rope coal my their cities
three tree with within eased fear ask fast trace case treks basin

oil oily turn take them regret agree vast civic read crew sweater
suit eight neighbor average decreased heirloom abstract own craft
signed opinion own deserve sufficient test defeated receive taxes

gwam 1' | 1 | 2 | 3 | 4 | 5 | 6 | 7 | 8 | 9 | 10 | 11 | 12 | 13 |

Punctuation Sentences

John Ran lives at 15 Lowe Street; Sue Reed lives at 17 Jo Street.
Ms. Mae Henning, an R.N., asked, "Did you answer a call on time?"
Jones & Brow, Inc. has the know-how to survive Monday (tomorrow).

Billy Smith, M.D., a member of the AMA, owes a pledge of $750.18.
Put the seven 1# bars of gold in the box--quickly, if you please!
Their P.C.s are: 100Mhz, 10.3G; 250Mhz, 8.2G; and 450Mhz, 15.2G.

gwam 1' | 1 | 2 | 3 | 4 | 5 | 6 | 7 | 8 | 9 | 10 | 11 | 12 | 13 |

TIMED

62. EMOTIONAL CONTROL
gwam 3'

In many cases, emotions involve strong feelings. Some peo-	4	50
ple have to make a special effort to control their emotions.	8	54
Lack of emotional control is sometimes observable on the job.	12	59
This lack of control is at times brought on by stress. Whatever	17	63
the reasons, a person should try to maintain control of emotions.	21	67
When emotions are out of control, a person frequently acts in a	25	72
way that is not acceptable to others. Lack of control may take	30	76
the form of complete withdrawal from ongoing activities or as an	34	80
outburst of outrage over some incident. A good rule is to remain	38	85
under emotional control at all times. In doing this, a person	43	89
serves as a role model for others who may have the problem.	46	93

gwam 3' | 1 | 2 | 3 | 4 |

63. PERSONAL QUALITIES
gwam 3' | 5'

Personal qualities are important to you in about any kind	4	2	47
of situation that may occur. These qualities are often stated	8	5	50
in broad terms like personality, skills, values, and attitudes.	12	7	53
These kinds of qualities also are often stated in a broad way as	17	10	55
good or bad. For example, if you come to your job on time and	21	13	58
work hard you are described as a "good" worker. Good personal	25	15	60
qualities may occur without much conscious effort, while others	29	18	63
not as good may need much work to improve them. Bad ones that	34	20	65
you may find that you possess are the most difficult to change.	38	23	68
In a more narrow sense, personal qualities are often based	42	25	70
on how you feel about yourself. The self-image that you have of	46	28	73
yourself is regarded as your self-esteem or self-respect. Varied	51	30	75
studies often reveal that the higher your self-esteem, the more	55	33	78
likely you are to exhibit success on the job. If what you en-	59	35	80
vision of yourself is high, then you frequently expect more of	63	38	83
yourself. If you feel good about yourself, you may also feel	67	40	85
good about others. If you have doubts about any of your per-	71	43	88
sonal qualities, rethink how you feel about your self-image.	75	45	90

Timed writings continued on next page.

gwam 3' | 1 | 2 | 3 | 4 |
5' | 1 | 2 | 3 |

SKILLBUILDING

Drill 2 •
Adjacent Keys

To improve accuracy, key each group of drills. If you make an error in keying a line, rekey that line one or more times. Repeat the drill as time permits.

FEATURE: Emphasizes two side-by-side keys.

BENEFIT: Eliminate adjacent-key errors.

TECHNIQUE TIP: Focus on smooth, continuous stroking.

GOAL: To key adjacent letters with the proper finger.

a for s; s for a

ask aspire cash rash ash aspect has task bash aspect aside basket
say said usage visa salty samples resale mesa satisfy sauna satin
Ask for usage of cash for the sample set aside in a satin basket.

e for r; r for e

era erased folder govern erode erupt linger fever were laser errs
real readily green premium read react bread prepares reduce relax
React to folders of paper that prepare for eroding of real areas.

r for t; t for r

art part article reports cart north heart start dart hurt cartons
try trust control tray extra transport trip retreat country trade
Try to transport the extra tray of art cartons to the north part.

i for o; o for i

lions iota iodine prior curious radio riots motion action furious
oil foil oink invoice ointment oily soil point doing choice joins
Actions in motion from choice radio stations were jointly foiled.

e for w; w for e

ewe newer hewed drew slews viewed fewer crews interview knew blew
wed welter sweat were weakly welcome weather western wetter sweat
We weltered an interview as newer, wetter weather blew out power.

o for p; p for o

open option proper ropes opposite opaque drop operate hopes optic
poet pocket poison coupon upon popular pole depot position police
Hopefully a proper coupon was deposited to open the popular pool.

gwam 1' | 1 | 2 | 3 | 4 | 5 | 6 | 7 | 8 | 9 | 10 | 11 | 12 | 13 |

Timed Writings
(3'- and 5'-timed writings continued)

64. OVERCOMING SHYNESS

gwam 3'

At times, shyness is the reason why people may appear timid, | 4 | 50
retiring, or reserved. These people often think they are shy. | 8 | 55
Shyness may seem to be troublesome, but shy people often live | 12 | 59
happy, normal lives. Most people tend to have a certain amount | 17 | 63
of shyness that others may or may not see in them. Most experts | 21 | 67
agree that it will help a person to overcome shyness by taking | 25 | 72
part in more social events. Some classes include the types of | 29 | 76
activities that often help people to overcome shyness. Examples | 34 | 80
are panels, role playing, buzz sessions, and discussions. To ap- | 38 | 84
pear before groups outside the class and to take part in events | 42 | 89
that involve meeting new people can help one overcome shyness. | 46 | 93

gwam 3' | 1 | 2 | 3 | 4 |

65. CLIENT SATISFACTION

gwam 3' | 5'

Whether you are in a merchandising firm with customers or in | 4 | 2 | 48
a professional or service firm with clients, a major reason for | 8 | 5 | 50
success is the satisfaction of people who use the goods and ser- | 13 | 8 | 53
vices of these firms. Most of the firms that have operated for | 17 | 10 | 55
a long time were built on slogans that expressed the desire to | 21 | 13 | 58
satisfy their clientele. Today, new firms that desire to succeed | 25 | 15 | 61
can learn much from many of the success stories of old firms who | 30 | 18 | 63
focused on their customers and clients. To satisfy customers in | 34 | 20 | 66
a competitive business world can be a real challenge. | 38 | 23 | 68

A key responsibility of all employees in a firm is to main- | 42 | 25 | 70
tain customer or client satisfaction. Potential customers or | 46 | 27 | 73
clients may sometimes be lost because of bad treatment upon the | 50 | 30 | 75
first contact with a firm. A bad attitude toward a firm can | 54 | 32 | 78
result from a very small incident that may not seem relevant at | 58 | 35 | 80
the time it occurs. Yet, the customer or client may perceive the | 63 | 38 | 83
incident in an entirely different way than does the firm. A firm | 67 | 40 | 86
needs to study the reasons why customers or clients are not sat- | 71 | 43 | 88
isfied and respond rapidly to retain them and to secure new ones. | 76 | 45 | 91

gwam 3' | 1 | 2 | 3 | 4 |
5' | 1 | 2 | 3 |

Drill 1
(continued)

Part G
Key one 2' writing on all paragraphs. Repeat. Try to increase speed on first writing by two gwam.

Note: If you have difficulty reaching your goal on the second 2' writing, rekey each paragraph as a 1' writing. Then try to reach your goal by rekeying a 2' writing.

Paragraphs—70% Balanced-Hand Words

gwam 1' | 2'

	1'	2'
When goals establish clear focus, they form maps for the	12	6
right purpose. The key to goal setting is to focus on the right	25	12
results and to form them for measuring or observing. The goals	38	19
are then visible for including the right blend at the level for	51	25
which they are established.	56	28
The element of quality is stressed greater than that of	11	34
quantity in writing of goals. An authentic goal that signals	24	40
reachable results helps to enrich the purpose of the goal. The	37	47
element of quantity is a problem when a rigid time for work is	50	53
not laid down.	53	54
To augment the right goals, it is usual to handle three	11	60
elements. Who is to reach the goal is an important element.	24	66
What span of work is required to reach the goal is another	36	72
element for inclusion. The standard then follows. The elements	49	79
enrich the chance for the right end result.	58	83

gwam 1' | 1 | 2 | 3 | 4 | 5 | 6 | 7 | 8 | 9 | 10 | 11 | 12 | 13 |
2' | 1 | 2 | 3 | 4 | 5 | 6 |

Part H
Key one 2' writing on all paragraphs. Rekey 2' writings until you reach your speed of Part G.

Note: If you have difficulty reaching your speed of Part G, rekey each paragraph as a 1' writing. Then rekey 2' writings until you reach your speed of Part G.

Paragraphs—50% Balanced-Hand Words

gwam 1' | 2'

	1'	2'
Consider work in several fields. It is important to select	12	6
the right field as you may spend idle time when you rush into a	25	13
position for life that may not be right for you. Protect your-	37	19
self against problems that are visible because such a rush	50	25
may hinder opportunities to enrich life.	57	29
You must have the right interest in work that is selected.	12	35
Spend realistic spans or quantities of time with information to	25	41
increase your knowledge about the right work for you. Profit or	38	48
title should not be the only signal. Place your sight on the	50	54
work which you want to do.	55	56
You should demonstrate the right ability for work that you	12	62
select. When you finally establish the plan for the work that	24	69
you desire to do, it is important to understand that you can han-	37	75
dle it. This is referred to as aptitude. You may then attain	50	81
the height desired when working.	56	84

gwam 1' | 1 | 2 | 3 | 4 | 5 | 6 | 7 | 8 | 9 | 10 | 11 | 12 | 13 |
2' | 1 | 2 | 3 | 4 | 5 | 6 |

Part 2

Intermediate Level Keyboarding

Section A — Skillbuilding Drills

FEATURE: Contains balanced-hand, one-hand, and combination phrases and paragraphs.
BENEFIT: Improve stroking rhythm.
TECHNIQUE TIP: Key phrases and paragraphs fluently.
GOAL: To build continuity and a smooth stroking rhythm.

SKILLBUILDING

Drill 1 •
Rhythm Drills

Part A
Practice each phrase using a smooth, snappy rhythm.

Balanced-Hand Phrases

do it/pay for/they paid/right angle/handle profit/visible signals
he is/but the/make them/audit panel/social theory/chaotic problem
go to/she may/turn down/usual vigor/eighth chapel/antique bicycle

of us/did rub/city maps/eight firms/island profit/skeptic auditor
by me/own spa/busy pair/ivory tusks/glairy enamel/suspend penalty
so if/cut hay/torn sign/shape bowls/orient sleigh/haughty rituals

Part B
See Part A.

One-Hand Phrases

at my/bet him/only read/avert waste/create better/average breezes
oh no/see you/oily pump/trade texts/assess facets/regrets opinion
be on/gas war/were fast/defer taxes/states agreed/sweeter dessert

no we/bad tea/join free/serve water/detect assets/greater reserve
my ax/car wax/data card/extra rates/savage beasts/regards estates
be in/saw red/beef stew/brave puppy/tested access/freezer drawers

Part C
See Part A.

Combination Phrases

as if/wet rug/best dorm/throw darts/enrich career/greeted visitor
am in/sad man/half case/their union/spends faster/audible reverse
or my/add jam/save fuel/after tight/excess height/sleight rebates

an ad/pin box/auto gets/draft title/secret ambush/million bushels
if my/big pup/eats fish/added focus/carved turkey/dormant acreage
or on/end was/sick crews/theme award/treats shrub/exerted torment

Drill 1 continued on next page.

Drill 1
(continued)

Part D
Key each set three times: first to improve technique, second to improve speed, third to apply concise control of finger motions.

Balanced-Hand and One-Hand Paragraphs

gwam 1'

Both of the girls ask for work in the firm downtown. The   12
man who may work with them, if they go to the downtown firm, can   25
aid them in the area they wish to work in.   He can handle prob-   37
lems and focus on the goals.   He will be a major aid for them.   49

The union staff agreed on extra wages for a baggage crew on   61
a barge.   The baggage crew earned far above minimum wages after a   75
year.   The union thus exerted a great degree of pull.   The crew   87
was then eager to pay union dues after the wages were in effect.   100

gwam 1' | 1 | 2 | 3 | 4 | 5 | 6 | 7 | 8 | 9 | 10 | 11 | 12 | 13 |

Part E
See Part D.

Balanced-Hand and Combination Paragraphs

gwam 1'

When she keys the form for their title on the new auto, go   12
to the city offices and make the payment.   When you are at the   24
eighth traffic light downtown, make a right-hand turn and travel   37
six blocks.   The city offices are to the right of the body shop.   50

You stress the usual opinion that a pupil needs to set a   62
career goal when starting a degree.   This decision may help a   74
pupil decrease wasted time.   The decision is often a hard one to   87
make and an option is for a pupil to start with core classes.   99

gwam 1' | 1 | 2 | 3 | 4 | 5 | 6 | 7 | 8 | 9 | 10 | 11 | 12 | 13 |

Part F
See Part D.

One-Hand and Combination Paragraphs

gwam 1'

If we can reserve extra seats, we may attend a debate based   12
on a fee decrease.   The debate starts after a short address.   We   25
read that you are only able to reserve seats at noon.   If we re-   38
serve these extra seats, we will look for you after the debate.   50

You must sign and mail the tax forms on Saturday.   If you   62
are late, the tax penalty may cause you problems.   You must as-   74
sess your personal assets and add each of the assets to the tax   87
forms.   You must also show assets of your firm and your acreage.   100

Drill 1 continued on next page.

gwam 1' | 1 | 2 | 3 | 4 | 5 | 6 | 7 | 8 | 9 | 10 | 11 | 12 | 13 |